Eddie can only speak through aggression. Kevin's shoes tap out his anger. Violent fights flare up between Eddie and Douglas: Julie hides under her desk while Jonathan calls into his inkwell for help and Kevin urges Douglas to kill Eddie.

Yet in the lulls between such destructive outbursts, Mrs. Craig perceives a real, if hesitant, sense of community emerging in the classroom. There are moments of celebration, as on the day that Jonathan, who believed he was a ghost and not a real boy, exclaims, "Doesn't it feel funny to wake up in the morning and say 'Who am I?' Doesn't it feel funny to wake up in the morning and be a human being?"

P.S. *P.S. Your Not Listening* is ultimately not so much a book about education as a book about love.

**ELEANOR CRAIG** continues her work with maladjusted children, and now lives in Westport, Connecticut, with her husband, author William Craig, and four children.

# P.S. Your not listening

# P.S. Your not listening

ELEANOR CRAIG



*Richard W. Baron / New York / 1972*

The names and identifying details about
persons mentioned in this book have been changed and
fictional names have been used instead.



FIRST EDITION



Published simultaneously in Canada
by Clarke, Irwin & Company
Limited, Toronto and Vancouver

SBN: 0-877-77034-4
Library of Congress Catalog Card Number: 77-185911

Portions of this book have appeared in McCall's.

*For Bill*

P.S. Your not listening

# CHAPTER 1

Douglas and his grandmother arrived first. Mrs. Grant was a heavy, weary-looking black woman wearing a shabby print dress and wrinkled elastic stockings.

"You Mrs. Craig? Well, Doug's here, but he don't want to come in. He's behind the door." A low groan from that direction. "He scared cause he wasn't allowed in no school last year. Some schools you've got! Can't even handle a nine-year-old." She looked at me disparagingly.

"Douglas." I peeked at the huge boy—all of one-hundred pounds at age nine—crouched behind the door. "Come choose a desk. You'll have first choice."

A louder groan.

"Boy," his grandmother pleaded, "your teacher here is talkin' to you. She wants you in that room. Now you git yourself up and git in there."

She reached down to pull him up, but he kicked her cruelly in the shins. "Ooooh," she swayed in pain, then leaned against the wall, eyes shut, biting her lower lip. Douglass grinned at her anguish. After a minute or two, she spoke softly. "You got the devil in you, boy. That devil sure in you."

"You got the devil in you boy . . . you got the devil in you boy . . ." he mimicked after her as she headed toward the exit.

Looking down at the handsome, brown-skinned child I was tempted to help him off the floor, but angry black eyes warned against it.

"It's time to come into our room now. I'll be waiting for you." Five minutes dragged by as I pretended to be involved in writing at my desk, and he continued to hide behind the door. Finally he crawled into the room as a baby would and sat on the floor before me, glaring. I stared in return at the untied shoes, the faded jeans, patched on both knees, the too-small blue shirt, bare belly bulging. I could look at his dishevelled form, but found it unbearable to maintain contact with his fierce eyes.

"Which—ahhh—which desk do you want?" It was a relief to find myself able to speak. "Since I had no idea you'd be so tall, we may need a bigger chair."

"Oh God!" he laughed and rocked on the floor. "Ideyah! Chayah! Ideyah! Chayah! Oh God, Oh God, what an accent! She can't even talk right. Ideyah! Chayah! Ha-ha-ha! Oh God, Oh God! You from Boston? You talk just like Kennedy!" He stood up at last. "Okay, I'll choose my chayah!" He picked up a chair and began to spin around, holding the chair out with one hand.

I headed toward him. "Put that chair down!' He twirled faster and faster. "Can't you see? Oh gosh, what a nut! What a nut! I am putting it down!" The chair shot out of his hand and slammed against the wall, leaving its impression on the cork bulletin board.

"Dizzy," he sank to the floor. "Dizzy, mmmm, dizzy," he murmured. I leaned against the wall, grateful for support. I'd had one student for ten minutes but already felt as if I'd been through a long and harrowing day. As I watched him roll on the floor, I thought of the meetings at which his problems had been described. Nothing had prepared me for this.

Douglas had been one of fifty children screened for this pilot class for the socially and emotionally maladjusted. An important qualification had been waived in order to admit him. The admissions committee—composed of a psychiatrist, three social workers, principals and teachers—had originally stipulated that no child be accepted unless his parents agreed to participate in whatever treatment might be recommended and be available for weekly conferences with the school's psychiatric social worker.

In Douglas' case, this was unrealistic. His young unwed mother had first given birth to a severely retarded child Luke—and less than a year later to Douglas. When Douglas was four, she suddenly called the welfare department to say she was leaving her children.

By the time the caseworker arrived at the housing project, Douglas was leading his retarded brother from unit to unit, in search of their mother. Neighbors supplied the information that she had left with another woman's husband.

Luke was sent to a state institution for handicapped children. Douglas spent two years in what proved to be an excellent foster home. Though he had grieved for months for his mother and brother, Douglas' social worker felt that he had made a good adjustment. Finally a welfare worker made contact with their maternal grandmother in South Carolina. When she realized the children had been abandoned she came north to make a home for the two boys.

But at six, this second major upheaval was too much for Douglas. He became disruptive in school and unmanageable at home.

In the second grade he had bitten and kicked his classmates several times and nearly stabbed one child with scissors. The principal finally was forced to exclude Douglas from school. After that he had a "homebound" instructor, paid by the city to provide one hour of tutoring daily in the homes of children unable to attend class.

Despite his tragic background, Douglas' intelligence measured in the near superior range. Yet the prognosis was guarded. Hopefully he would adjust to our small class and eventually move back to a regular classroom. Otherwise the purpose might be purely diagnostic, to determine whether his disturbance was so profound that he would have to be removed from his home to a residential treatment center.

As Douglas continued to roll about on the floor, the one other member of my class—Kevin Hughes—appeared at the door with his mother. They both froze in horror at the sight of Douglas writhing on the floor.

I tried to smile encouragingly. "Mrs. Hughes, Kevin, I'm Mrs. Craig. And this is Douglas Miller. Would you like to see our room?"

Kevin's mother was a large-boned, austere woman in a mannish brown tweed suit. In contrast, her son had a delicate, sensitive face, soft blond hair, and timid brown eyes. Although he was eight he looked closer to five. The psychiatric evaluation described him as depressed and withdrawn.

"All right, son. That's your teacher, Mrs. Craig, and here's a place for you." Her large hands on his tiny shoulders, she maneuvered him into the nearest seat. "Pay attention. Don't forget your lunchbox. I'll be waiting when the bus brings you home. Good-bye, Mrs. Craig." She looked again at Douglas, this time with unconcealed disgust, and hurried out.

Kevin looked at neither of us. He sat rigidly with his hands folded in his lap and his head bent down. These boys had been described to me in psychological terms, but no one had suggested the incongruity of pairing so frail a child with such an overpowering classmate.

Douglas sat up now and looked at Kevin. "What's wrong with this teacher? She's retarded probably. Didn't even tell us to put our things away." He swung open the coat closet. "I'll take the first hanger. This is the other kid's." He stared at Kevin.

Kevin rose obediently, almost mechanically, and hung up his jacket. But with incredible speed, Douglas grabbed the jacket, darted across the room, and hurled it out the window. He turned to face us triumphantly. Kevin looked away. Infuriated that his victim did not react, Douglas was at his side before I could stop him. He shook Kevin's chair violently, succeeding in dumping him onto the floor. "Oh gosh, what a nut! Are you retarded or something? Get outta my seat." Kevin moved to another seat. His face was expressionless.

"Douglas," I began, "you will not be allowed to—"

"Hold it," he interrupted. And he now sat down calmly, hands folded in model schoolboy position. "Okay now, I can't work, see? I get all shook up. So what are we gonna do here?"

I decided to forget the jacket for the moment and began again. "Let's start with introductions. I'm Mrs. Craig." The yellow chalk squeaked on the green board. M-R-S . . . C-R-A-I-G.

Douglas pounded his fists on the desk furiously. "Oh wow! Don't you even know that Mrs. has three s's in it? Can't you hear them? MiSSuS! MiSSuS! Maybe they spell it that way where you come from, but you better learn it has three s's in this part of the country."

"We'll spend time on spelling later, Doug. The first thing is to learn each other's names. Now would you like to draw pictures of what you did this summer?"

"Are you kiddin' Would Macy's tell Gimbel's?" he yelled.

"Calm down, Doug. Kevin hasn't had a chance to talk since he got here."

"Heeyuh! Heeyuh! Oh God!" Douglas slapped his forehead in despair. "It's heRRRe! Call this a class? With a retarded teacher?"

Douglas then spent the rest of the morning dismantling the toy closet, enthusing over each discovery, trying out each piece of equipment, then discarding it for another. By noon the floor was littered with crayons, trucks, punching bags, and Lincoln Logs. Despite my encouragement, Kevin would not leave his chair and continued to sit with his head bowed, even when I pulled up a chair beside him and tried to talk with him.

He was uncomfortably overdressed in a starched white shirt, large bow tie, and stiff new corduroy pants—all of which gave him the appearance of a wizened old man. Kevin's record contrasted sharply with Doug's. He had never been excluded from school. In fact, it was to his teacher's credit that he had been referred to guidance at all. He was so passive and withdrawn that a less perceptive teacher might have described him as a "terribly good boy, one of the quiet kind who never get into trouble." Fortunately, his second grade teacher had recognized him as a maladjusted child and set into motion the procedures to get help for him. She had done this despite great resistance from his parents, who insisted at first that although he was not like other boys, he had no emotional problems.

Neurological tests revealed nothing organically wrong with him despite his history of convulsions as an infant. Psychological tests indicated low-normal mental ability, but the tester acknowledged that Kevin's score undoubtedly was adversely affected by his depression. The psychiatrist reported that "without treatment, Kevin's feeling of inadequacy and lack of nurture might develop into a schizophrenic process."

He was the only child of a middle-aged couple who had married late in life. From a previous marriage, which had ended in divorce, his mother had a twenty-year-old son, now in the Army. His father was a burly man, built like a wrestler. He described his desire to have a "real boy"—one who would play Little League baseball, be a football hero in high school, and someday work with him as a mechanic.

Instead Kevin had had a difficult infancy. He not only suffered several convulsions during his first month, but also developed many allergies that required frequent hospitalizations for dehydration and other complications during his first year. There was no way to determine whether his illnesses and early separations from his mother were so traumatizing that his ability to relate was impaired, or whether his parents were unable to accept this scrawny, ill baby and deprived him of their love from those earliest days. Whichever way it began, after initially denying such feelings, both parents admitted that he had never brought any pleasure or satisfaction into their lives.

Though he rarely cried, he never laughed or smiled. None of the neighborhood children would play with him. At home he spent much of his time sitting on the floor in a corner of his room silently arranging and rearranging a set of small plastic soldiers.

I wondered if Kevin would be more approachable after he began his sessions with Ceil Black, our psychiatric social worker. She would be seeing both boys individually each week. Then every Friday after school, she and I would confer.

I wished we had agreed to meet that first day rather than at the end of the week.

Before lunch, Douglas made his first trip down the hall to the boys' bathroom. Kevin shook his head when asked if he wanted to go. There were a few minutes of peace, suddenly broken by the angry voice of the custodian. I looked down the hall in time to see Mr. Jakowsky chasing Douglas, both running at full speed. It was the first of many times that Douglas hurled wads of sopping toilet paper to the ceiling of the bathroom where it stuck, as somehow he knew it would. Douglas dashed past me and fled into the coat closet. Poor Mr. Jakowsky, now chagrined at his own behavior, turned and limped away, muttering softly.

At lunchtime, Douglas gobbled his entire meal while Kevin was still meticulously spreading a yellow napkin over his desktop. "Hey kid, let's see what you've got." In a disarmingly helpful way, Douglas unwrapped Kevin's sandwich, then sank his teeth into it. "Ugh! Salami!" He spat the entire mouthful into Kevin's lunchbox.

No reaction from Kevin. "That's enough!" I yelled, starting after Douglas. He led me several times around the room, then took off down the hall.

I refused to satisfy him by giving chase. It was a relief that he was gone. Perhaps I could draw out Kevin a little. "What would you like to do this afternoon, Kevin?" No answer. "Play a game?" A barely perceptible nod. "Hear a record?" Another silent no. "Then let me read to you." If he heard the story, his frozen face gave no indication. Only once did he take a surreptitious glance at the book.

We didn't see Douglas for the rest of the school day, but his timing was superb. Exactly at dismissal time, he sauntered in, collected his jacket and lunchbox, and waited at the door. "I'm first in line."

"But you weren't even ready to stay with us today! Tomorrow you must not touch Kevin's lunch. You must remain in the classroom."

He looked at my face as if he were considering these demands, then lowered his eyes. "I could bite your tit you know."

When Doug and Kevin were gone, the principal peeked in to say good-night. Carrie Silverstein was a tiny dynamic woman, whose brother and two sisters held prominent university positions.

She had rejected her opportunity for similar advancement in order to provide continuity of leadership at this difficult school. Ours was the only special-education class in the building, but the district included many economically deprived families. Her devotion to her job was almost legendary among the teachers. They talked about how, during her hospitalization a year before, she had called school constantly, even on the morning of her operation. The night she was released she came in at ten o'clock, just to check the building. Some griped about her unannounced crayon and workbook inventories, but she was never deterred by fanaticism for detail from putting emphasis where it belonged. She was always available to counsel a new teacher, calm an upset child, encourage a poor performer. This time, I needed her.

"I can't even get started with these two. Workbooks or play therapy—they're not ready for either. What shall I do?"

"You can't expect to start either right away. But workbooks might be part of the therapy."

"But I'm so concerned about these boys being together. I understand the theory of an aggressive child and one who's withdrawn balancing each other. But when I see this in practice, it seems as though we're just setting Kevin up to be victimized."

"It's too soon to tell anything. I'm betting you're in for some surprises. Anyway, it won't help to have you brooding about them. Now go home to your own."

My own, my own. Ann would already be home. Junior High was out at two. Still with luck I might beat the elementary school bus and arrive before Richard, Bill and Ellen.

But traffic was heavy. It took twenty minutes just to cross town, and I was stopped at a light at three-thirty, exactly when their bus was due. Although my husband was at home, I was upset at not being there to greet them myself, on their first day back to school. I imagined them calling me. It's the inescapable guilt that makes working hardest for a mother, I thought, finally turning down our narrow drive.

I could see Richie and Billy in the yard playing football with several friends. Billy waved and yelled hello, but Richie broke from the huddle and ran toward me, jumping the hedge that bordered the lawn.

"Hey Mom. Guess what! I get to play soccer this year, but I've gotta get a gymsuit. The coach says we have to be ready if we want to go out on the field tomorrow."

I knew that another school year had begun for sure when I saw that both boys were wearing their new shoes, now completely scuffed and muddy. "In the house, both of you," I called, "and change your shoes."

The other players moaned and flopped down on the grass to wait out the interruption. "Hurry up, you guys," they yelled as Richie and Billy raced into the house.

Richie was now in fifth grade and Billy was entering third, both at the same school where they'd started kindergarten. Their teachers and classmates were familiar to them, and I expected no major problems. My youngest, Ellen, was beginning second grade and for weeks had been expressing fear that she would find the work much harder than in first.

My main concern, though, was our oldest girl, Ann, thirteen, and suddenly so pretty. All summer she'd become increasingly apprehensive about entering junior high. She and her friends talked about greasers, jocks and hippies—groups representing the rumored junior high caste system.

I followed the boys into the house. Ann and Ellen were standing at the kitchen counter, sharing a cellophane bag of pretzels.

"Mom, Mom, I got Mr. Spitzler, the worst science teacher! Everybody hates him. He's so unfair. And we've already got three chapters for tonight. Can't I be changed, Mom? I'll flunk, I know I will!"

Ellen stared in amazement at the horrors of junior high Ann detailed. She would never be able to find her locker, every hall was lined with hundreds. She'd forget the combination. There were long walks to each class. She was sure she'd be late.

But the recital ended with the advantages of the cafeteria. "We get chocolate milk, ice cream sandwiches, all kinds of good stuff."

I smiled. Ann would be all right.

Finally, seven-year-old Ellen got to talk. Her teacher gave prizes for each finished workbook. Robin, her best friend, was in her room again, after all. They were afraid they'd be separated.

Having heard the excited voices, Bill came down from his study and joined us at the kitchen counter. "Annie, would you put the coffee on? And what about mother's first day?" Bill had to stoop to kiss my forehead.

"Ya, Mom. Tell us about your kids. What are they like?" Ann asked, as she filled the kettle.

"I think I have to sort the whole day out before I can talk about it. I feel sort of numb. To give you an idea, the custodian chased one of my pupils down the hall."

I expected some sympathy, but they all laughed, and then it seemed funny to me, too.

The kids all decided to bicycle to the store for school supplies, and I was glad for the chance to have a quiet cup of coffee with Bill. I worried about him. He looked so thin in his rumpled chinos and baggy navy sweater. His dark hair and beard had become almost totally gray since he'd begun writing full time, almost a year ago.

His original plan had been to lead a double life, working all day as a salesman, writing his history book evenings and weekends. But as his research on the Second World War progressed, the need to travel and devote full time to it became urgent. Luckily, I was able to return to teaching. Our income was severely reduced when Bill left his job, but we had no regrets about the gamble we'd chosen to take.

Bill took a second cup of coffee back upstairs while I raced unsuccessfully to finish the laundry before dinner. After a quick meal, there were more dishes, more laundry, ironing. When the kids were in bed, I went up to Bill's tiny office in what had been the attic. One wall was eaved so that he could only stand up straight in half the room. The one window, with a lovely view of the tall pine trees at the side of the house, now was black. The glass reflected Bill's tired intent face as he hunched over the typewriter.

His filing system consisted of stacks of yellow legal paper and books intricately arranged all over the floor. No one but Bill entered the room. I stood in the doorway.

"Ready for bed, dear?"

"Boy, am I," he said, stretching his long arms over his head. "I feel like I could sleep forever."

I felt that tired too. Yet when the house was finally in darkness I lay in bed restlessly. Why, I wondered, were my last thoughts of stranger's children and not of my own.

# CHAPTER 2

We made no progress toward an academic program on the second day. Douglas started the morning by spinning in circles until he fell from exhaustion. I made a mental note to ask the social worker whether I should have tried to stop him. Kevin again sat silently and responded neither to Douglas nor to me. Efforts to involve them, in listening to a story or playing a game aggravated both Douglas' aggression and Kevin's withdrawal. When there was any pressure to conform, Douglas would run out of the room. He had left the building and was spinning out on the playground when the mothers arrived to pick up their kindergarteners. Fearing a scene, I approached him and caught his hand. "You belong in our room," I said sternly.

"No, no!" he yelled, and suddenly flopped down on the blacktop, pulling me down with him. Mothers hurriedly grabbed their children and began to run, staring back at us. I struggled up and gripped his hand so tightly that he was forced to rise, screaming, "You've broken my hand. Why? Why? You've broken my hand!"

At the door I discovered that Miss Silverstein had witnessed this drama. She engaged me in a whispered conversation. "You'll have to contain him in the classroom or we just can't have him here. It's too dangerous to be responsible for children who leave the building."

"I know, but how?"

"He's testing you. Why don't you gamble that he really wants to be here, and tell him that if he leaves the room he may have to stay at home for a while?"

The second day's lunch was almost a repetition of the first. Kevin was still setting his food out when Douglas took the apple and cookies from Kevin's desk and munched on them arrogantly. Kevin nibbled listlessly on his sandwich, dropped most of it into the wastebasket and brushed invisible crumbs from his desktop.

"Douglas, you may not continue to take Kevin's lunch. His mother packs it for *him.*"

"Boy, the trouble with this teacher—she always wants her own way. Gosh, what a nut."

After lunch we toured the building, visiting the nurse, the library, and even taking a look at the enormous furnace in the subbasement. Our last stop was the custodian's supply closet. "We may want to come in here to borrow a broom or wash out paint brushes."

"Wow, that's boss!" Douglas enthused, and I turned just in time to see him slam the door. The lock clicked before I could grope for the knob. We heard Doug's laughter, then his receding footsteps. I fumbled unsuccessfully for an electric switch, not even sure that there was a light in the small closet.

Kevin began to whimper.

"It's all right, Kevin. Doug is just playing a trick on us. You help me call for Mr. Jakowsky." I yelled for the custodian while Kevin's sniffles developed into full sobs. No one came.

"Dark, dark," he cried.

"Don't be afraid. The dark can't hurt us. Someone will come soon." I reached for his thin shoulder but he shook my arm away. My efforts to comfort him seemed to increase his anxiety.

"Dark. Where's Mommy?" he whimpered. "Where's Mommy?" I pounded on the door for a few moments, then became reconciled to the prospect of waiting until we could hear someone approaching the closet before we in turn could be heard. Kevin's sobs were now reduced to gasps. "Dark, ooooh, dark."

"We can sit down and wait. Someone will come soon." He sank to the floor. I could hear him sucking his thumb. I sat too, and he edged closer. "Douglas is bad," he said. "I hate Douglas." Frustrating as the situation was, I felt encouraged that Kevin had finally begun to express himself. I put my arm around him.

"Maybe you and I can help him to be better."

"No! He's bad!"

"We can stop him. We can show him that he can't tease people anymore."

"No more teasing," and he leaned against me, sucking his thumb furiously.

We sat this way about twenty minutes, then both jumped as light suddenly flooded into the little closet. Mr. Jakowsky had come for a mop and was as startled as we were. "My God, what's the matter here?"

"Don't worry, Mr. Jakowsky. It was just Douglas playing a trick on us." I guided Kevin back to the room, aware that the custodian was staring after us.

Douglas, his feet up on his desk nonchalantly, was chewing on the remains of Kevin's sandwich, which he had retrieved from the wastebasket. "Oh! Where you been?' he asked, his eyes wide with innocence. I needed a few minutes to decide how best to handle the morning's disaster. My anger at Doug's behavior was tempered by the realization that because of it I had at last begun to establish some rapport with Kevin. We accomplished in forty minutes what might otherwise have taken months.

"Doug, Kevin and I have decided that we are not going to let you—" He rushed to the wastebasket and spat out a mouthful of Kevin's sandwich. "Ugh, this has lettuce in it!"

"Now," Kevin's voice was wavering, "now you have to bring me a treat tomorrow." Douglas turned sharply to stare at Kevin. "And you owe me an apple too." I exulted. Good for you, Kevin! "Kevin's right, Doug. It's wrong for you to take his lunch."

"Will you turn off the water hoses? Will you? Some people just don't like Africans. There's always some persecutor, someone like you, getting other people into trouble."

"Wait," I said. "You've been getting yourself in trouble. Why not stop and think of what will happen before you do something?"

As he headed for the bus, he rotated his index finger around the side of his head to symbolize my insanity.

On the parking lot he turned to face the school and shouted back, "You are crazy, you know! You are really crazy! Some class, two crazy kids and a crazy teacher!"

The two crazy kids and the crazy teacher had come together in anticipation of a new state law which would mandate an educational plan for socially and emotionally maladjusted children. There were few guidelines. I was undecided whether the class should be a permissive therapeutic environment or a structured learning situation. Two closets reflected my dilemma—one jammed with teaching materials, a controlled reader, prepared tapes and worksheets, the other brimming with blocks, puppets, a punching bag, and finger paints.

After the children left I sorted through the equipment, wondering how best to utilize it. It seemed impossible that either boy would be ready to learn much in the months ahead. What had once sounded so logical, balancing a withdrawn child with one who is acting out, now seemed a grave mistake. Douglas would use Kevin as a pawn, pushing him ever deeper into his retreat.

On one of the shelves I found the box of notes I had accumulated in preparation for this job. The top papers detailed guidelines used in establishing our pilot class. I reread the first page:

> Criteria to be used in determining the eligibility of pupils and special class placement: 1. A definition of the socially and emotionally maladjusted child for special class placement: A. His social and emotional disturbance prevents him from profiting from his regular class educational experience, and/or his behavior and attitudes are disturbing to his classmates or group because of his problem. . . .

I stood at the closet, scanning through the papers as far as page ten, which listed seven qualifications for the ideal teacher. I read the first two:

1. Able to take lack of achievement without resorting to pressures or feeling personally threatened.
2. Able to accept many kinds of unusual behavior while maintaining control, without being punitive. . . .

"While maintaining control"—I thought of Douglas' locking me in the custodian's closet. What made me think I could handle disturbed children?

I remembered first learning about the program at Hosmer School, where I had taught the year before. Marie Collins and I were having coffee in the faculty room and read the notice on the bulletin board.

> Department of Special Education seeks master teacher for Pilot Program with socially and emotionally maladjusted children. Please contact Jim Hanley, department head.

"Who'd want that job?" Marie remarked.

I didn't try to explain to her the excitement I felt at that moment. I had always loved working with children. I enjoyed teaching, but knew, without ever having considered special education before, that this was an opportunity and challenge I wanted to pursue.

When I told Bill about it that night, his reaction was similar to Marie's. "But why?"

"Honey, don't you see? It's my chance to learn without going back to school. Besides, when have I ever had a class with no disturbed children? To teach them separately, where their behavior wouldn't disrupt twenty-five others would seem like a privilege!"

"Maybe." He didn't look convinced. "But with four children of your own, I'm afraid you'll find it too demanding. Please don't rush into it."

I thought about it for days, wondering most of all whether I would be considered qualified. Finally I made an appointment to see Jim Hanley.

"As yet there's no specific teacher training for this type of class," he said, "but the person we're looking for must have certain characteristics which don't necessarily accompany a degree in psychology or education. We need someone with insight and acceptance.

"Furthermore, don't pursue the job if you're looking for a sense of personal gratification. Challenge, yes, and a wonderful learning experience working with other professionals to return these kids to regular classrooms. Gratification, no."

I left his office feeling that position was the ultimate challenge in teaching. For weeks, members of the Transitional Class Planning Committee interviewed me and observed my classes. Two months after the first meeting with Jim Hanley, I received a letter from him. I found it now in the stack of papers.

Dear Mrs. Craig,
Welcome to Guidance and Special Services!

Bill and I had celebrated at Mario's the night it arrived. "Congratulations," he'd lifted his glass in a toast. "I hope it won't be too tough."

Too tough. Nothing in those interviews had prepared me for a child like Douglas. I put the papers away and realized with a start that it was four-thirty, an hour after I'd told my own children I'd be home.

I was learning to use the drive home as a period of mental as well as physical transition, forcing myself en route to switch thoughts from the classroom to my waiting family and their needs, needs often as basic as what to have for supper.

But every night, regardless of whether the evening had been hectic or relaxed, I found myself lying in bed unable to sleep. Always, I wrestled with the same question, "Tomorrow, how can I be more effective with Douglas and Kevin?"

# CHAPTER 3

Ann's bus came at seven-thirty. I fixed a pot of coffee for Bill and packed lunches for the other kids and myself, then drove Rich, Billy, and Ellen to their bus stop.

"Hey, Mom," Billy suggested as we were leaving the house. "Those kids in your room. Would they like a surprise?"

"Like what, Bill?"

"You could take my guppies. The mother is having babies again."

About a half hour after the boys arrived, Douglas finally became too dizzy to spin around anymore. They both were intrigued by the fish, especially when they heard that the guppy was pregnant.

"She's having babies because she's so sexy," advised Douglas. "Kevin, do you know what sexy means?" Kevin blushed, pressed his nose against the fishbowl, but did not answer.

"He's retarded, I guess. Say, Mrs. Craig, do you know what screw means?"

"Well—ahh—mmm, a screw is like a nail with threads."

"Dumb! Dumb! She's really crazy!" He threw an eraser violently against the closet, then tore around the room, flinging every object he could grab. Chalk, a plant, books, the blotter and papers on my desk all sailed through the air. Kevin took refuge by crouching in the kneehole of my desk. Douglas threw the fish food, and the box broke open when it hit the blackboard.

"Ha! Now she'll be hungry! She'll be so hungry she'll have to eat her babies!" Douglas ran into the closet. Next, I expected, the coats would shoot across the room. I was not prepared for the silence. It took a minute to discern his muffled sobs. He was huddled in the corner of the closet, in fetal position, crying heartbrokenly.

I approached and he kicked out violently, so I sat on his desktop and waited, not knowing for what. I felt myself flushing, angered by my own ineffectiveness.

Kevin continued to cower under my desk. Douglas wept more openly. Ten minutes. No change. Fifteen minutes. Kevin ventured a quick peek at me. Doug's sobs were becoming less frequent. Twenty minutes. A small voice from the closet.

"I could buy some food."

"What?" Startled, I was afraid I hadn't heard correctly.

"I could buy some food next Saturday."

"The fish won't live until next Saturday, Douglas."

Silence. Then, "I have an idea."

"Oh?" I walked toward the closet, and Doug rose to meet me halfway.

"I could sweep it up."

I wanted to hug him and cheer him on as he labored to Scotch-tape the box back into shape. At the same time, I felt certain I must watch quietly, accepting his action as if it was the expected course.

Kevin did not conceal his amazement. He crept from the shelter of my desk and stared openmouthed as Douglas spent the rest of the morning brushing every visible grain of fish food into the battered container.

I didn't know how it had come about, this miraculous change, but for the first time I felt hopeful about Douglas.

On Friday, Douglas arrived late, holding a greasy paper napkin across the palm of his hand. "Damn stove, Damn stove. Can't make anything on that damn stove. Look!" There was an ugly red burn, glistening with margarine. "Just wanted an egg for breakfast." He was fighting tears.

"This must hurt terribly, Doug. You must feel like crying." He did cry then, allowing me to put an arm around him and comfort him until the tears subsided. We sent for Mrs. Rogers, the nurse, who led him to her office for treatment.

Kevin as usual had been a silent observer. He sat at his desk, holding out his hand to me. "Look," he pointed to an invisible wound. "I hurt my pinger. I hurt my pinger!" I hugged him, pleased that he was seeking the attention Douglas had received. "Too bad, Kevin, too bad. You and Doug both have hurts. Let's find a toy, and maybe it will help you forget."

With unusual enthusiasm, he opened the toy closet and rummaged through a box of small toys, emerging with a plastic baby bottle. He headed toward the door. "I get wa-wa. I pill it. I pill it." He hadn't spoken in baby talk before, and I felt a little uneasy about it. I was at my desk when he returned. "Up, up." He climbed into my lap, closed his eyes, and sucked on the bottle. Though unsure of the value of permitting this behavior, I nevertheless hesitated to interrupt any opportunity to improve our relationship. He quickly drained the bottle and hurried out to the bathroom for a refill.

"Wock me. Wock me." He dragged over the child-sized rocking chair. I managed to wedge one hip into the little wicker seat as he climbed back on my lap. This time he positioned my hand to hold the bottle for him and lay his head back on my shoulder, sucking contentedly.

Douglas, his hand now bandaged, walked in on this bizarre scene. He stared at us and went straight to the closet. Next, Douglas too had a bottle and was on his way down the hall. Oh no! Not both of them! But when he returned he hesitated at the threshhold, then threw the bottle to the floor. The nipple shot off, and the water spilled out. He stared at the wet floor, then hurried back to the closet and took out paste, scissors, and a handful of paper. Kevin was not even aware of Douglas' presence. Douglas seemed not to want to interrupt us, yet he frequently glanced uneasily in our direction as he cut and pasted.

It was an enormous relief when Kevin drained the second bottle, but once again he returned for a refill. This time I spotted our social worker in the hall and motioned for her attention. "Pssst!

Ceil! Quick! Kevin is on his third bottle! Do I give him a quota?"

She laughed. "Let him go today. See what he wants to do. We'll talk about it after school."

More rocking and sucking. But Doug, now totally exasperated, lifted the sticky paste brush from its jar, approached us, and ran a wide streak of paste up Kevin's back. Kevin didn't even notice. He remained a baby all morning. Frustrated, Douglas took apart the entire closet, while muttering about the crazy teacher and the retarded kid. I hoped to bring Kevin back to reality by frequently commenting, "It's fun to play baby, isn't it?"

Douglas finally approached me cautiously. "I'm hungry," he said, looking down at the floor.

"Why don't we have lunch a little early today, Kevin?" I said. "You and Douglas can get ready right now."

But I had been too abrupt. Kevin looked startled, then climbed down and crawled over to the hand puppets which Douglas had scattered on the floor. He put on the rubber crocodile and returned to devour me, first my arms, then my face. The attack was accompanied by ferocious growls. "The crocodile's pretty angry at me," I said.

Douglas grinned. "You sure are blowing your stack, aren't you kid?" He laughed uneasily as Kevin's crocodile turned menacingly in his direction. "Look kid, you can be mad, but you don't have to be that mad. Cut it out and I'll let you have all your lunch today." Kevin growled and snapped. Douglas was unnerved. This time, he pleaded. "Why don't you stop it? You're bugging me, man. Turn it off. You can have half my cake if you turn it off."

Surprisingly, Kevin responded. He dropped the puppet and sat at his desk. I went to Doug's side. "It was kind of you to offer to share your cake."

"That's okay, nothing to it." He carefully pulled the waxed paper from the sticky dessert and broke the chocolate cupcake in half. "Sorry I don't have no forks or nothing, but hands were made before forks weren't they?" He ceremoniously deposited a piece on Kevin's desk.

When he finished eating, Douglas spent the afternoon putting away all the toys he had scattered earlier, stacking them neatly in the closet.

Kevin just sat, ignoring Doug's offering, unresponsive when urged to try a taste. As the bus arrived he mashed the cake flat with both palms and left it on his desk. Douglas looked more hurt than angry. Neither answered when I wished them a happy weekend. Douglas started down the hall beside Kevin, then returned to our door as if he had forgotten something. "Wow!" he whispered in a confidential tone, beckoning me to lean down. "He sure is a harsh kid, isn't he? He's a harsh kid. You better start getting hard on him."

Ceil came in as soon as the boys left. I launched into a long recital of the week's events, anxious for her advice. but unwilling to let my monologue be interrupted until everything had poured out—Douglas locking us in the closet, taking Kevin's food, running out of the room, and by contrast the insight and sensitivity of some of his comments; Kevin's timidity, his inability to express feelings verbally, his unexpected baby-playing. And finally all the questions in random order: "Is it harmful to allow Kevin to play baby, or will it help him? When Douglas begins to spin, should he be allowed to continue until he falls? Would it be better to try to stop him first? How much should he be allowed to get away with before he's punished? What is an appropriate punishment? Do you believe there is any hope that either one will ever really be well, Ceil? Do you think it's possible? Either one?"

Her first response was simply a smile. I was to learn that she used pauses in conversation more effectively than most people used words. Ceil was an honors graduate from Simmons with a master's in social work. She and her lawyer husband had a twelve-year-old son. Because of her outstanding record in her department, she had been assigned to this pilot program, for which she had suggested the name Transitional Class. Now she focused her wisdom on its teacher.

"Think back to when Douglas and Kevin were first being considered for the class. Don't you remember how negative the child guidance people had been about our accepting Douglas? They felt that he needed residential treatment and that our taking him might just be delaying his chance of getting it. How could you expect anything but a long hard time with him while he tests you out? He has no reason to trust you or anyone else. Even your story about his cleaning up the fish food shows more remorse and sensitivity than we had any right to expect him to reveal. About the spinning—it's something we often see in schizophrenic children. Once they are involved in an activity like this, there can be a break from reality. They repeat and repeat the same action over and over again, unaware of their own repetition, unable to stop themselves. I'm not sure that Doug's spinning means that he is persevering in just that way. But if you want to bring him out of it, words won't do. You'll have to interrupt him physically. Touch him. Put your hand on his shoulder and lead him to something else."

We were sitting in the low wooden chairs at the round "reading table." Her reddish curls bobbed and her face became paler as she spoke more intently. "Look, if you didn't keep questioning yourself, you wouldn't be right for this job. But you can't assume the guilt for their problems. The damage has been done over a period of years. We won't undo it overnight.

"As for Kevin, finding comfort and security by being a baby is serving a purpose for him. He may want to do it again. Your assuring him that it's fun to *play* baby was fine. Next time he sucks, you could talk to him about babies, how they learn to crawl and then to walk and talk, to play and do all the things a boy his age can do. This will help in easing him back to the present and in recognizing all he has accomplished since those early days. I've made a tentative appointment for us to see his parents next Thursday evening, okay? It's the only time the father could make it. It should be very interesting to learn more about what goes on with Kevin at home. See you at eight on Thursday."

We parted, only to meet unexpectedly twenty minutes later rushing into the same supermarket.

# CHAPTER 4

Bill was now hoping for a spring publication date and worked the whole weekend, emerging from his study only for meals and what seemed like constant refills of his coffee mug. Ann had looked forward all week to the first slumber party of the school year. She spent all day Saturday packing and repacking her case, changing her mind each time about which nightgown she wanted to take, choosing records, and trying in vain to convince Bill to let her borrow his tape recorder. It seemed that whenever he came down to the kitchen, Ann was there waiting: "Please Daddy! Can I?"

Sunday, Richie had a Cub Scout meeting at our house. There was a noisy debate on the different ways of raising money for an outing, and an even more animated exchange over where they would go when they had the money. Once, as I passed by the living room, I heard Richie say modestly that he didn't think even a car wash *and* a bake sale would raise enough for a trip to Yellowstone.

The weekend passed so quickly, I had no time at all to reflect on Ceil's suggestions. But I began to appreciate how very important it was that those who work with exceptional children have a fulfilling life of their own. By Monday, Friday's despair was long forgotten.

I began the week with enthusiasm, and a determination to establish a definite program. Art seemed an appropriate starting point—no right or wrong, no books to remind one of past failures, just the pleasure of working with the materials. Before the boys arrived I set up two easels, each with an assortment of paints.

A minute after the bus door slammed, Douglas came bounding into the room. Forgetting his ritual spinning, he approached the easels immediately.

"Oh, painting, huh? I'm very good at it. I never got a turn before, but I'm a good painter."

Kevin finally entered, head bowed, shuffling as if he were sleep-walking. Mechanically, he put his lunchbox and sweater in the closet and took his seat.

"Hey, Kevin, ya gonna sit there looking mean all day? Trying to spoil other people's fun? Well, man, I'm painting."

Douglas made a huge red O, then smeared the paint all over his paper and discarded it for another. He became more and more gregarious as he repeated the O and then the smearing with one color after another.

Kevin submitted to Doug's prodding by approaching the easel, but wouldn't try to paint. Finally I put my hand over his and together we brushed dabs of color on the large paper. Left on his own, he continued woodenly, with no apparent pleasure.

Douglas was thrilled with his paintings.

"Man, isn't this boss? I'm taking mine home tonight. Not because I don't wanna leave them here or nothin', but I'm gonna plaster them all over my walls. Okay?"

Douglas was having a great time. By eleven-thirty he had produced twenty-three paintings, now scattered all over the floor to dry. But Kevin had given up, returning to his desk in a maddening state of apathy. Despite my coaxing, he remained at his desk the rest of the morning.

"It's almost time for lunch, Doug. Why don't you just finish up the picture you are working on?" I said.

Picture was perhaps an inappropriate word. One paper was all red, another all black, the next a combination of both, and so on with other colors.

"I'm too busy to take a break, thanks," responded the artist.

For once, Kevin could eat without Doug's interference. He spread the usual yellow napkin on his desk and began to unscrew the cup from the thermos.

"Can't drink," he muttered, "can't drink."

"Oh? Something wrong?"

"Can't drink." His hands groped inside his desk. He brought out the baby bottle, secreted there since last week's episode. He poured the milk from the thermos to the bottle. "Dwink, dwink."

Doug looked at Kevin, then wildly splashed paint all over the easel. "That kid's at it again!" he moaned.

"Wock me!" Kevin begged.

I hoped Ceil's advice would be of some help as, once again, I jammed one hip into the little rocker. He was on my lap instantly, sucking loudly.

"It's fun, isn't it Kevin, to pretend that you're a baby again. Being held and loved, sucking a bottle." He closed his eyes. His mouth worked vigorously on the nipple. The milk was nearly gone.

"Then remember, Kevin, how babies learn to do more things—to creep and crawl all around, discovering everything. His toys, the legs of a table, the color of the floor, it's all new to the baby."

The milk was gone. He sucked in air.

"Then the baby gets bigger and bigger and bigger. He begins to pull himself up and then to stand alone."

His mouth relaxed. He was listening. He slid to the floor, crept to the legs of his desk, and, holding on cautiously, pulled himself to standing position.

"So finally the baby becomes as grown up as you, Kevin, and able to do so many things." He smiled.

"Are you two through?" Douglas bellowed. "Man, you make a person feel like a gutter. Nobody speaking to you, everybody stepping all over you. Like a gutter."

He poured the paint down the legs of the easel, one color after another, then shook the final drops of the last can into the fishbowl. "There! If she dies, will it be my fault? Well I hope she does and her babies too! You can probably hate me."

"Doug, you're unhappy because you thought we were ignoring you. I'm sorry it seemed that way. Now quickly take the jar and fill it with water. We'll transfer the fish."

Douglas didn't answer. He was curled up in the closet again, crying as he had before. Kevin hurried off to the sink to fill up the jar.

We scooped the guppy out with his thermos cup. Once in clear water, her recovery was remarkable. I tried to let Douglas know, but his sobs were louder than my words.

"Here, Kevin. Keep the jar on your desk. You watch her while I go down the hall and rinse out her bowl. She can't be in the jar too long."

When I returned, Kevin had the guppy on his desk. He was chopping her to pieces with his ruler.

Sickened, I grabbed the wastebasket and with the ruler whisked the sections of fish into it. Kevin kicked the desk over, then crushed the rolling crayons and pencils with his feet.

Douglas rushed from the closet and grabbed Kevin by the collar. "You sure have a mind for killing, boy! You sure have a mind for killing!" He punched Kevin in the face. Amazingly, Kevin stuck out his tongue!

"Enough!" I shoved them apart. "Enough hurting each other! No more hurting anything or anybody! It's all right to be angry, but *say it!* Stop hurting each other!"

Douglas yelled back. "He's wiping his sweat on us! Are you gonna let him keep on killing?"

"Look, we are here to form a class, to learn together. We've made mistakes, but from now on. . . ." This time my efforts were being drowned out by the beginning of what I was later to call Kevin's "shoe language." As I spoke, he tapped and then stamped his feet louder and louder.

The bus came. When the boys left, it was my turn to cry.

During the next few days, Douglas' moods were extreme—wild tantrums, sudden crying spells, or expressions of such unexpected insights that I would be encouraged until the next disruptive episode. Working with him became exhausting and disheartening. His resistance was even greater when I tried to introduce academic work. I planned to start by sitting with each boy individually, using an easy-to-read library book. Each time, he knocked the book from my hands, then slumped to the floor feigning sleep, sometimes for half an hour.

Kevin, who had so much he needed to express, now relied on his shoes to do it for him. Every time I approached him his feet would begin to tap—heel, toe, heel, toe, louder and louder. I said he must stop so that we could read. Tap! Tap! Tap! He looked at me blankly, then shrugged innocently. He was being very good but could not be expected to control those disobedient shoes.

The shoes became more and more expressive, interrupting whenever Kevin wanted to interrupt. On Thursday, when it was his turn for "work period," he headed for the fountain outside the room.

"Just a minute!" I called. "You may have your drink when we have had a look at this book."

He eased out of each shoe and carried them into the hall, carefully lining them up directly under the water fountain, then in stocking feet returned to his desk. Kevin was obedient—only his shoes were defiant.

I kept the appointment with Kevin's parents Thursday evening. But it was difficult to rush out after supper—even harder when Bill demanded, "How often is this going to happen?"

Ceil and I arrived at the darkened school simultaneously. It felt strange to be the only ones in the huge building. While we waited for the Hugheses, I filled Ceil in on Kevin's recent behavior. They finally arrived twenty minutes late, offering neither explanation nor apology.

We squatted on low chairs around the reading table. Ceil took the initiative. "Mrs. Craig and I feel that Kevin is adjusting to this new situation about as well as we would expect at this time. We are still getting to know him, which is one of the purposes of his being here. Therefore, there is really not too much to share with you at this point, but we did want to open up the channels of communication between home and school with this first meeting. Perhaps you will be able to tell us more about Kevin's behavior at home."

Mrs. Hughes, again wearing the same man-tailored suit, eyed Ceil suspiciously. Mr. Hughes, who looked much younger than his matronly wife, wore a stylishly tailored teal-blue suit and pale blue tie. His wavy brown hair was slicked back, his face so boyish and unlined that it looked unlived in.

"We also felt," Ceil continued, "that you might have some questions you would like to ask."

"Do I? Oh boy, do I!" Mr. Hughes plunged in. "The kid hasn't come home with homework once! Is he doing anything in this place or not? What's going on here? Is he learning anything? What the hell kind of school *is* this?"

Ceil jarred my stunned silence. "Mrs. Craig can answer questions about the learning program better than I."

"Yes. Well, ah, part of the reason Kevin is here, Mr. Hughes, is that he does have a learning problem. But there is more than that. I am sure you remember some of the things the psychologist discussed with you after he had seen your son and tested him. When he is able to work, Kevin will receive individual attention here and progress at his own rate. We have to work together to help him reach that point of readiness."

Ceil elaborated on Kevin's feelings of inadequacy, and the importance of cooperation between home and school in helping him to overcome his problems.

Mr. Hughes shook his index finger at Ceil, then at me. "I get it! I get what you two are telling me! You're saying the kid hasn't got it, huh? From what you're telling me, my son just doesn't have what it takes to make it in the real world. Right? In other words—*he might as well be a teacher!*" And, grabbing his wife by the arm, he left the room.

# CHAPTER 5

Ceil and I postponed our usual Friday conference in order to attend a meeting of the Transitional Class planning committee. This group, formed over a year before, had been charged with the responsibility of finding a location for the class, hiring the first teacher, and determining with what age group the program would begin. This had been a difficult decision.

Three years earlier, Mr. and Mrs. David Beecher had realized that the city could offer no educational plan for their son. Donald was nine at the time and had been diagnosed as both severely disturbed and neurologically impaired. While looking for help, his parents discovered that there were many other children who could not attend regular classes yet did not belong in programs for the retarded. The Beechers formed a parents' group which pressured both the local school board and the state legislature for action.

The board, receptive to the parents' plea, made an investigation which showed that at least one hundred children in the city had problems that could not be handled in existing classes. This estimate did not include the retarded, for whom classes were provided. But a pilot program could accommodate only five or six.

Where to begin? After lengthy study and consultation, the committee agreed that the logical and most hopeful start would be with the younger children, ages seven to nine. Their emotional and learning problems were not yet compounded by years of failure and frustration academically, nor complicated by trouble with the law and the community, as was the case with some of the older children.

But Donald Beecher was almost thirteen now, and the committee had to inform his parents, who had paved the way, that their son was too old to be included in the first class for the socially and emotionally maladjusted, our Transitional Class.

Not until two years later did the state legislature finally enact a public law mandating education for all children, regardless of their handicaps. Many states still have no such provision.

Donald Beecher had to wait. And the committee listened as the social workers and teachers described more than fifty young children they hoped to place in the program. Some were given high priority. A waiting list quickly formed. There were long discussions about the composition of the group. What kind of children would benefit most by being together? Could the class be balanced by mixing the withdrawn with the so-called acting out?

Names were removed from the list when a few parents protested that special-class placement would stigmatize the child.

The meeting on this first Friday in October was called to review the top two cases on the waiting list. Douglas and Kevin were about to have new classmates.

The committee now included head of special education, Jim Hanley, chief social worker Barbara Rizzo, Arlene Wood, the psychological examiner, a junior high school principal, Miss Silverstein, Ceil, and me.

We met in the conference room of the Administration Building. Mr. Hanley explained that the committee was anxious to add more children to the class and asked whether I thought we were ready. I briefly summarized some of my experiences with Kevin and Douglas. "Perhaps four will seem more like a class and make it less difficult to establish a routine. It's hard to anticipate how the two boys will react." Then Ceil read the case histories of each new boy.

"Edward Conte is a seven-year-old with a background of behavioral problems since kindergarten. He had a severe separation problem, and although his mother was able to leave him by November, he still cried much of the morning. The kindergarten teacher reported that he was unmanageable, restless, provocative, and disobedient. He could not sit still even for a story, and picked fights constantly.

"His first grade teacher wrote, 'He cannot go more than a few days without attacking another child. It seems as if he just explodes for no reason.'

"Parents of Edward's classmates finally petitioned the principal for the boy's removal, complaining that their children were afraid to come to school. He was excluded in February and placed on homebound instruction. Although Edward was on the waiting list for this program, the principal tried him again in a regular class this September. He was even more assaultive, and stayed less than a week. Mrs. Rizzo spoke to the parents about his being included in the Transitional Class."

Mrs. Rizzo took over. "I saw Mr. and Mrs. Conte individually and together. They are both extremely immature people with no understanding at all of the seriousness of Edward's condition. The marriage has always been stormy, and they are constantly on the verge of terminating it. The mother was three months pregnant when they married. She was eighteen, and he was just twenty. There is a five-year-old sister, who so far seems to be doing all right in kindergarten. The father works in a gas station and says he spends all his free time on his motorcycle. The mother wants to enroll in a local modeling school and is annoyed that Edward is not in school because she does not have her freedom. Miss Knight will tell you about the testing."

"Edward's verbal I.Q. was 105, whereas his performance score was 92, barely average. There was a sense of inappropriate social knowledge and poor ego structuring. There have been some academic gains, but he appears to be at the mercy of his emotions."

"In summary," Miss Knight read, "this is a child with ego disturbance and poor impulse control."

"For your purposes, Eleanor," Mrs. Rizzo turned toward me, "I would recommend that if Edward goes into your class, you will have to adjust all demands to his very short attention span."

"Any questions?" Mr. Hanley asked.

I was shuddering at the thought of Douglas and Edward together, but didn't want to admit it.

Perhaps Ceil read my expression. She said, "Of course one of our goals is to maintain a balance in the group. For that reason we had hoped to add two girls to the class at this time, but the waiting list is made up almost entirely of boys."

"Let's hear about this other boy," Mr. Hanley said.

"The next case is that of Jonathan Bergman," Ceil continued. "He is an extremely disturbed eight-year-old, who is also reacting to his parents' destructive handling. Jonathan is an only child, born after his parents had been married for six years. At the time of his birth the mother was twenty-six and the father thirty. After having Jonathan, Mrs. Bergman suffered three miscarriages. She had a two-month hospitalization for a mental breakdown after the third miscarriage, and the doctor had advised them not to try again. Recently, she began private treatment with Dr. Gross, who feels that she is a borderline schizophrenic. She goes on periodic alcoholic binges. Apparently, the husband is solicitous only when she is incapacitated. Otherwise he is cold to both his wife and son. The father is a very successful businessman, vice-president of a large ad agency. Spends very little time with his family."

"It's interesting, isn't it," Jim Hanley interrupted, "how some of these guys can function so well on the outside and be such miserable failures at home? Is Jonathan in school now?"

"No, he only lasted a few weeks in first grade," replied Mrs. Rizzo. "He really couldn't be contained, both because he was so disruptive and because of encopresis. He soiled daily." I gulped.

"Miss Knight tested him," Mrs. Rizzo concluded.

Miss Knight read from a manila folder. "The WISC, Wechsler Intelligence Scale for Children, reveals high average ability, but I do not feel that that is a true measure because his anxiety interfered with his performance.

"Psychological testing indicates that this child's behavior is a reaction to many inner fears and great insecurity, to such an extent that he is unable to control his fantasies of destruction. Nor can he separate them from reality. Life must be frightening for Jonathan."

"There's one positive factor we don't want to overlook," Ceil added. "That is, that both parents desperately want help at this time both for themselves and for their son. They are all going to be seen regularly at the Child Guidance Center."

Jim Hanley replied, "Even so, I frankly think this kid may be too sick even for our program. But in that case, including him will be diagnostic. If he can't make it here, we won't have much choice. Yet I wouldn't want to recommend a residential placement at his age until we've given this a try."

The committee voted unanimously to accept both Edward and Jonathan on a trial basis.

Driving home, I thought about how little academic progress had been made in our class. Now there would be two more pupils. Of course, it took time to "establish relationship," but had we even begun? And where were we heading?

On Saturday, Billy and Ellen walked to the library with me. While they chose their books, I hunted through educational material, hoping for some helpful techniques. One book looked promising, *Educating Emotionally Disturbed Children* by Haring and Phillips. Beside it was a title I shall never forget, *Emotionally Disturbed Teachers in the Public Schools.*

The Haring and Phillips book was so full of ideas that I became excited at the prospect of trying some. The authors compared permissive programs to ones that were highly structured, concluding that the more rigid setting offered security and achievement to children with problems. The goal was to establish a system of built-in consequences and rewards, which would at first be imposed by the teacher but should, in time, lead the children to self-discipline.

By Monday morning I was prepared to utilize many of the book's suggestions, but first the two boys had to be told that they would soon have new classmates. Kevin had no reaction, but Douglas seemed concerned and asked repeatedly, "Are they black or white? How old? How big?"

Nothing could have united Douglas and Kevin more than this news. "Let's keep our desks away from them, Kev. Just you and me are buddies."

"No. My big brother can be your friend," Kevin said. "He's the best one. If you don't believe it, come over sometime."

"Can I? When can I come over, Kev, huh?"

"Maybe soon. I'll ask my mother."

"Today we are going to do something new," I interrupted, handing them both folders. "These contain work for each of you, work you will be able to do. I'll sit with you first Kevin, then with you, Doug, to answer questions. As soon as you finish a paper, I'll correct it. If you are completely done by lunchtime, we can use the gym this afternoon."

"Hey, that's boss! Come on, Kev, let's hurry up!"

Kevin shook his head. "When I hurry, I make mistakes."

"Now listen, dummy," Douglas counseled, "it's all right to make mistakes. Everybody does. Some people say there's no such thing as mistakes. Like in the South they say that, but man, have they made mistakes!"

Douglas finished early. Kevin barely was through by twelve. The textbooks were so right about "anxiety-binding" activities! Both had been attentive and cooperative all morning.

After lunch, as the promised reward for a productive morning, we went down the hall to the gymnasium. We began tossing the basketball, but when Kevin caught the ball he refused to return it. "Right here, Kev old buddy," Douglas called.

"Uh-uh." He clutched it tighter. "I only play alone. I never play with anybody."

Douglas pointed to the corner. "You stand over there, *pleeeeze,* Mrs. Craig. Kevin and I have to do our physical fitness. Kevin," he demanded, "get over here!" I was ready to interfere for Kevin, but surprisingly he followed Douglas to the middle of the court. They threw the ball back and forth. Whenever Douglas missed a catch, he would command, "Go get it!" And Kevin would run after the ball until finally he was exhausted and slumped against the wall, his face white, his blond hair dark with sweat.

Douglas approached him. "Hey, look, it's been a good day. Now, don't mess it up."

"Kevin looks tired, Doug." I left my corner. "And it's later than I realized. We just have time for drinks before the bus."

Douglas playfully slapped Kevin's back. "Good game, buddy." Poor Kevin nearly collapsed.

"Me and Kev are gonna live together on a farm someday, Mrs. Craig. Right, Kev? We don't have to get married to get our food cooked. We can do it ourselves. We can be bachelors."

As soon as they left I hurried to the office to inform Miss Silverstein that I had found the secret to success—a structured program.

# CHAPTER 6

By previous arrangement, their mothers brought Edward and Jonathan a half hour early the next morning. Mrs. Bergman, Jon's mother, was prematurely gray at thirty-seven and looked closer to fifty. Her nose and cheeks bore the telltale blotches of alcoholism. Two buttons were missing from her stained tweed coat.

Mrs. Conte, Eddie's mother, was young, only in her mid-twenties. Her jet-black hair was elaborately teased on top and hung almost to her waist in back. Her heavy mascara and pale frosted lips presented a ghostly effect. Her long fingernails were coated with bluish silver polish.

The two women waited uncomfortably while their boys chose closet spaces and storage cubbies. Then Jonathan's mother murmured good-bye and scurried away. Her son looked bewildered and frightened.

Eddie clung to his mother's suede jacket, begging her to stay. She grabbed his skinny wrists. "I'm sick of you actin' like a baby!" She stormed out angrily.

He wailed for almost ten minutes, then stopped abruptly. By the time the bus arrived, the new pupils were sitting quietly.

Douglas and Kevin must have rehearsed their song on the way to school. They sang to the tune of *Three Blind Mice.*

Two new punks
Two new punks
We hate them
We hate them
We hate them and they hate us
We hate them and they hate us
Two new punks.

Jonathan's pale cheeks flushed. He closed his eyes tightly and covered his ears with the palms of his hands.

Kevin and Douglas launched into a second chorus as they defiantly dropped their coats on the closet floor.

Jonathan was a heavy-set boy, several inches taller than Eddie, but it was the smaller boy who became the aggressor.

He darted at Douglas, leaping on his back from behind, as if for a piggyback ride. Douglas was thrown off balance, and fell over backward. He and Eddie rolled around the floor, legs locked, arms flailing. Kevin peeked out from the closet. "Kill him, Doug, kill the punk."

They tumbled across the room, now in a half nelson, until both bodies struck the burning radiator. Howling in anguish, they fell apart. Douglas, lying on the floor, raged through clenched teeth. "Okay, Mrs. Craig, you did it. You let this little killer in."

But it was my turn to be angry. "And what did you do, Douglas? And you too, Kevin." He stood at the closet door. "Did you give them any chance at all? I'm sorry that we couldn't have—"

"Sorry isn't gonna help my back now, is it?"

"Fuck your back!" Eddie screamed.

Douglas sprang up and grabbed a chair. "I'll kill him. I'll bash his head in. It's your fault, Mrs. Craig—egg—Mrs. rotten egg."

"Enough! This is a place for learning, not for fighting—" This time I was interrupted by Kevin's feet. Tap-tap, heel-toe, heel-toe, tap-tap-tap. Then both feet slammed against his desk, tossing it upside down. The contents rolled out.

Douglas patted his ally. "Okay, okay. I don't blame you for being mad, boy. I hate her too." Kevin stamped on a pencil, splintering it.

"Why don't you control it, pal?" Douglas pleaded.

Kevin crushed a green crayon with his shoe. He ground it into the tile.

"Come on, man. You're blowing your stack again, aren't you? Look, I'll give you the best of everything I've got, except my milk. Let's get away from the punks."

Douglas carried his desk to the corner of the room farthest

from my desk. "Come on, Kev. You move too. We can sit up here together. We won't need to have no dealings with those guys."

Kevin slumped forward limply until his head rested on his knees. Douglas became impatient. "Now look, I told ya we're moving, dummy." He picked up Kevin's overturned desk and pushed it beside his own, then dragged Kevin's chair, with its occupant, to the same location.

I helped Eddie up. "Look," he pointed. "Look at them babies, hiding in the corner. Huh! They moved their things, so I'll move mine!" He did, jamming his desk against mine—a silent plea for protection.

Douglas whispered to Kevin, now and then turning around to point to one of us.

Jonathan was left stranded in the center of the room. His face was red, and he was grimacing with obvious strain. From the odor, I realized his predicament. "Let me show you where the bathroom is, Jonathan. I'm going to help you so you won't have that problem here."

"Oh no, no thanks. It's just goose grease. You see I was using goose grease to make a new formula with diaper powder and water. Don't come any nearer! If you do I'm going to blur my vision! I can't stand people with faces like yours."

I opened the windows, then handed Douglas and Kevin their folders, expecting vehement protests. They not only accepted the work but concentrated on it all morning, although they remained in seclusion.

There were no folders for Eddie and Jonathan today because I wanted to work with them and get a clearer idea of their abilities. But each time I tried to approach Jonathan, I set him off. "Don't come any closer. My radar has picked you up. Pow, pow!" I spent the morning with Eddie, while Jonathan crossed his eyes, muttered, and whistled.

We ate lunch together in the classroom, as we had each day. No one responded to my attempts at conversation—it was *food* they wanted. Silence except for the sipping and chewing. The peaceful, satisfying interlude lasted almost twenty minutes, then Eddie stamped on his empty milk carton, making it explode with the sound of a shotgun. This triggered a chain reaction. When everyone had popped his milk carton, I advised that cleanup would have to be quick, since we were going to have a film in the afternoon.

Jonathan was still eating and mumbling. I bent down to him. "Are you talking to me, Jonathan? I'm afraid I can't hear you."

"Oh no, no. Just talking to my banana."

"Can bananas talk?"

"He likes me to talk to him."

Jonathan lingered by the shelves after he had put his lunchbox away. I moved close enough to listen.

"Now you stay right where I put you." He sounded anxious. "What? Oh no you don't! No jumping out! That's right, don't move, act like you're dead."

"Lunchboxes don't move by themselves, Jonathan. It will be here until you move it."

He rolled his eyes and shrugged my hand off of his shoulder. "Whew! Jeez! You don't know anything!" His eyes filled with tears. All afternoon he shot nervous glances at the metal box.

I had prided myself on choosing such an appropriate activity for this occasion: a guidance film called *The New Classmate*. Since no one else looked approachable, Eddie was delighted to be chosen for all jobs. He threaded the projector, pulled down the screen, and turned off the lights.

"Kevin and Doug, if you move your chairs back a little you'll be able to see the screen," I suggested.

"Man, is she crazy! The trouble with her is she always wants her own way."

"Tell her," Kevin whispered.

"You've just brought in two little punks. Don't speak to us anymore, after what you've done."

Jonathan continued talking to himself. Eddie bent over the projector, intrigued by the film's progress through the machine. I alone watched the pictures, which showed how many small acts of kindness had made a new pupil feel welcomed by the other children.

Every day, for the rest of that week, Jonathan soiled and burped, Eddie and Douglas fought, and Kevin and Douglas continued their self-imposed exile. Yet there were glimmers of progress. Folders were being completed by lunchtime, with the understanding that only then could one participate in the afternoon activities—painting, playing a game, or listening to records. We had finally established limits, rewards, and consequences, a necessary step toward self-discipline.

Miss Silverstein came in after school while I was working on folders. "Sorry I can't give you more notice, Eleanor, but the central office just called. Jim Hanley is coming over tomorrow to visit your class with some people from Belmere."

"Oh, who?" I asked.

"They wrote saying they're interested in setting up a similar program there, and Mr. Hanley feels we must accommodate administrators from other areas who'd like to observe. They'll probably arrive around nine-thirty. I have no idea how long they'll stay."

I thought of the constant upsets we'd been having since the new boys had arrived. "Wish me luck."

"Mazeltov," she smiled.

# CHAPTER 7

Eddie's entrance the next morning didn't augur well for visitors. Running in ahead of the others, he leaped around the room screaming, "I didn't even see him! I didn't even see him hit my mother, and now her head's all lumpy! I hate him! I hate him! I'll never call him my father again. I'll just call him uncle. Oh, oh, my mother's head is broken, and he's gone! He took his things and left. When he comes back I'll hold the door so he can't get in. If he smashes it down, I'll stab him with a knife."

Kevin and Douglas arrived together. "Do it, go ahead," I heard Kevin whisper.

Calmly, Douglas strolled over to Eddie, held his shoulder, and belted him in the stomach. The impact completely winded Eddie. He doubled up on the floor clutching his stomach in anguish, then began crying hysterically.

"Douglas! How dare you?" I demanded, rushing to the stricken child. "How dare you walk in here and hit him?" I cradled Eddie's head. "And Kevin, what's your part in this?"

Douglas pointed at me indignantly. "Now listen, you keep quiet, because you don't know what you're talking about." He shook his finger at Kevin. "And you shut up too. I don't need no advice from you. That little punk on the floor cried all the way to school about his mumma. It's embarrassing."

After the speech, Douglas sat down and devoured his lunch. Kevin's smirk revealed his pleasure at Eddie's misery.

Eddie was still sobbing when Jonathan began to yell. "Oh it's here now. It followed me to school! All night it kept me awake! Hurry! I have to get it with my atomic radiation gun. Pow! Pow!"

Eddie began to shout again. "He left before I woke up! I didn't even see him go. He left. I was asleep. I was asleep. I didn't hear the fight at all, and then that pisser Doug has to sock me! Oh, oh."

His head was still in my lap. I brushed back his dark hair, damp from the tears. "Mrs. Black will be seeing you at ten today. You'll be able to tell her about the problem. I guess it made Doug angry to see you cry on the bus. But he's going to learn soon to tell people with words and not with punches."

"Ha!" Douglas licked the frosting on his cupcake. "That little punk's too dumb for conversation!"

Eddie sprang up, fists ready to fight, then thought better of it. "Huh! Mrs. Black thinks I'm waiting till ten o'clock for her, she's crazy!" He ran down the hall toward her office.

The visitors suddenly stood in the doorway. My boss, Mr. Hanley, introduced me to the three men from Belmere: the head of special education, a guidance counselor, and a principal. The four took chairs in the back of the room. The children became unusually quiet.

We had progressed to the point where each child would work on his folder of assignments while I sat with one after another at the round table, giving individual instruction in reading and arithmetic.

After explaining each child's folder, I called Douglas over to the table. Today he would start fractions, using red felt circles cut into thirds and quarters. He got the sections confused. "I don't get it. This is junky stuff."

"Think of it as a pie, Doug. One is cut into three pieces, the other into four. Each person will have one-fourth of this one and one-third of the other."

"Mmmm, a pie, huh? I'll have it, thanks." Smacking his lips, he stuffed each piece of felt into his mouth, then pretended to gag and choke, dramatically clutching his throat, until he spat out the last scrap. "Man, what a crummy pie! Why didn't you say you're a lousy cook?"

"Man, what a funny student." I couldn't resist it. "Why didn't you say you're a comedian?"

Douglas felt obliged to protest. "Help her, God." He looked

at the ceiling. "She's trying to crack jokes in a foreign language. It's you'RRRRe, NOT yah!" But he seemed pleased and put every bit of felt in the wastebasket.

"It's moving again!" Jonathan was bent over, staring into his desk. "Where's my gun? Pow! Pow!"

Eddie jogged in and circled around the room, gasping. "She's not there. Mrs. Black's not there. Am I supposed to wait for her all day?" He was distraught.

"She'll be here soon, Eddie." I had to yell to make him listen. He stopped running. "She always comes. It's not quite ten. Sit down for a few minutes."

It didn't work.

"I'm getting all the stuff outta her room. She's not using it with anybody else! I'm not waiting for her all day." He left.

A moment later, Ceil Black peeked in at his empty chair and silently mouthed the question "absent?" I pointed toward her office. She nodded and disappeared.

I looked around. Douglas had settled down and was working on his folder. He liked the system of checking off each assignment as he completed it. The first pupil finished had first choice of the afternoon activities. He responded to the challenge. Jonathan did not. Again and again he would draw a dot with his pencil, then enlarge it, bearing down harder and harder. Incredibly, he managed to drill holes through his entire workbook. I had learned that words would not reach him. He had to be touched, physically interrupted. "Jonathan, how are you doing?" I put my hand on his back. He was startled. I slipped the ruined workbook off his desk and replaced it with anagrams. "How many words do you think you can make before lunch?" He began rummaging through the letters.

Kevin was scribbling on his papers. Although he had been given short simple assignments, he was unable to work independently. "Our time to work together, Kevin." I led the way to the table. He shuffled along behind.

"You seemed to be having trouble with the arithmetic. Let's start again." Just having someone beside him, he was able to complete the assignment that had been so frustrating moments earlier. The contrast in papers was astonishing. "Finished al-

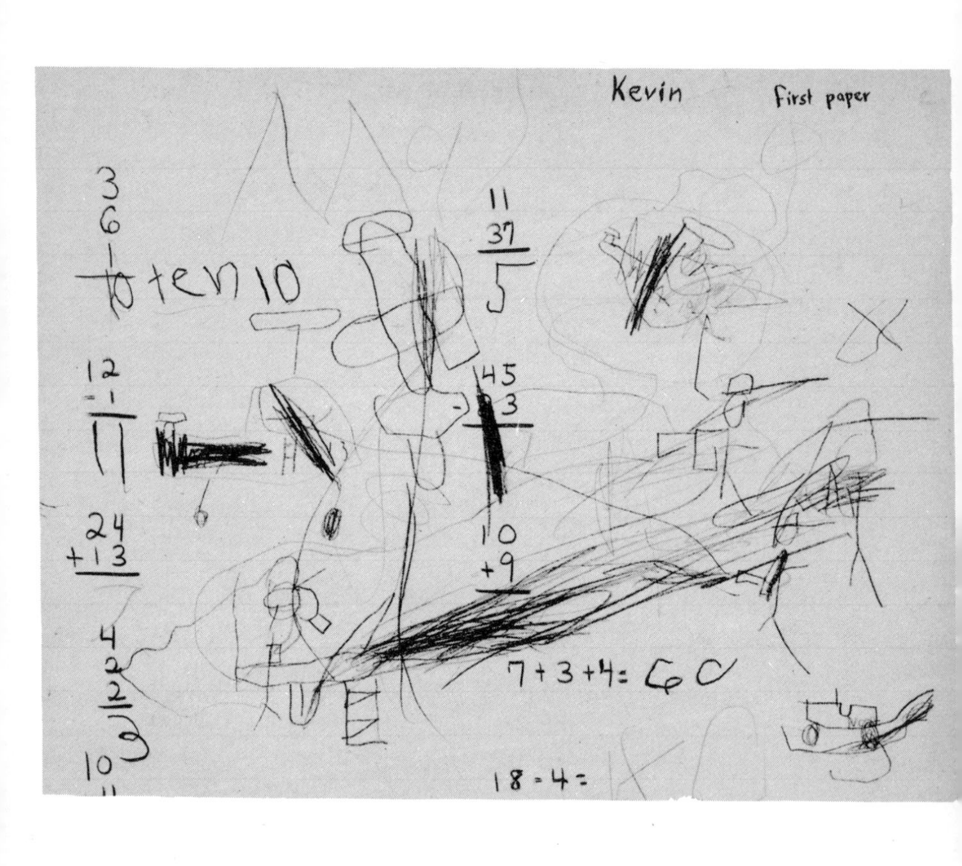
Kevin
first paper
ten 10
7+3+4=
18-4=

Kevin

2nd paper. completed right after first paper

Kevin

3
6
1
10

12
-1
11

4
3
7

1
2
2
3

11
37
48

45
-23
22

10
+9
19

7+3+4=14

18-4=14

ready, Kevin? And they're all correct! It must make you happy to have done such a fine job."

He tried to conceal it, but a smile broke through.

I looked back at the visitors, hoping they had caught Kevin's fleeting expression. They were smiling too. Mr. Hanley winked.

Douglas broke the mood. "Where's Eddie? I'm not working while that little punk's having fun. I'm getting him now."

"You know the rules about leaving the room."

"Shut up, shut up. I'm getting him, I told you."

"It's Eddie's turn with Mrs. Black now. Remember that yours is at twelve. You won't want him to interrupt you." I spoke in a whisper, anxious that my words would not force him to save face by openly defying me.

"I could kill you," he whispered back. But he sat down! At eleven Eddie returned from Ceil's office with a sketch of his battered mother and several finger paintings. His time with Ceil had been obviously an outlet for his tensions. He was still edgy but in much better control. He opened his folder.

"Do you think I'm gonna do all this?"

"Do you think you are?"

He started right away.

Ceil came for Jonathan, who became self-conscious walking past the visitors. "Whew—burb—urp, I think I'm blowing my top! Whew! Here I go! Here I go!" She guided him out, a hand under his elbow.

Douglas finished his folder and began playing with anagrams. With Mr. Hanley observing, I was grateful that Douglas was so engrossed. I stretched to get a glimpse of his words. So far he had EDDIE

A<br>
T<br>
SHI

"It's almost lunchtime, Kevin. May I correct your folder?" He slumped forward on the desktop to conceal his work.

Jonathan burst in, carrying three Play-Doh monsters he had molded in Ceil's office. Jubilantly, he arranged them on his desk.

"Hey Ed," Kevin taunted, "Jonathan used the Play-Doh. I thought that stuff was just for you."

Eddie exploded. He knocked over Jonathan's desk, picked up one of the monsters, and hurled it against the wall. Jonathan bawled.

"That bitch!" Eddie screamed. "I told her everything is only for me!" He snatched the two other models and ran out. Once again, Kevin had provoked a furor without being a participant. He smirked. We could hear Eddie running toward Ceil's office, screaming, "Bitch! Bitch!"

I glanced at Jim Hanley. He rolled his eyes. The visitors shifted uneasily in their seats.

"You know, Kevin, I'm beginning to hate you," Douglas snarled. Kevin looked stricken. With great dignity, Douglas picked up the remaining Play-Doh and tried to push it into shape. He deposited it in Jonathan's hand, righted his desk for him, and bowed gallantly in my direction. "Okay, Mrs. Craig. Your turn to do something spectacular." Mr. Hanley and I burst into laughter. The children looked confused but joined in, even Jonathan.

Mr. Hanley glanced at his watch and rose. The four men nodded their thanks and filed out. I slumped down at my desk, relieved that they were gone. It was hard to imagine a worse day for having the Transitional Class observed.

By Friday of each week, I had compiled a list of subjects to discuss with Ceil. She in turn described her sessions with the children, interpreted some of their current behavior, and detailed any contact she might have had with parents.

My major problem today concerned Jonathan's soiling. "Why does he do it? What should I do when it happens, besides opening the window?"

We laughed, then she explained. "Jonathan's encopresis is his way of expressing his inner fears. Like Kevin when he taps, or Doug when he fights, Jon is asking us to listen. His symptoms speak for him. He needs to be freed from the manner in which he is revealing this anxiety, namely through bowel movements. We hope that in time the combination of his increased confidence in you, the success he will experience here, and the play-therapy sessions with me will reduce his tensions and enable him to express them more appropriately. Of course, I'll be working with his parents, but it's really the classroom that will be his therapeutic milieu."

"But for now, Ceil, the kids are beginning to call him names, and he becomes unbearable sometimes. What should I do?"

"What do you want to do?"

"I've been thinking about it. I want to send him home. Does that shock you? I want him to understand that soiling is unacceptable here."

"If that's what you feel, then do it. Just be sure he understands that you're not rejecting him as a person. Tell him calmly that he's not ready to be in school that day, but you hope he will be able to stay tomorrow."

Then we discussed Eddie and the violence he witnessed at home. We agreed to set up a conference with his mother as soon as possible.

I showed Ceil the papers I have saved. Jonathan's ghost family, which he drew on each day's folder, had Mommy telling Daddy that Junior was bad (wet pants), and she had put him underground with King Tut's coffin. Doug's stories, illustrated with magazine cutouts, were hard to read but very moving. Eddie drew himself swallowed up by a menacing-looking mother. Kevin's angry scribbling was done the day Jonathan and Eddie joined us.

We talked until four-thirty. "Incidentally, save those and any other interesting papers," Ceil said, slipping into her coat. "They'll be helpful when we discuss the children at the clinic. See you next Friday. Happy weekend."

"You too."

began → ONE ← (began)
Lovely
Day
Mrs
coss
Was
Loney.
She
HaD
to
KNow
What
Hapen
to
Mr
coss.
he
haD
Ben
IN
the
War.
A
Year

HaD
Past
AND
WhiL
She
Was
WalKING
AND
Befor
She
COLD
Say
Yipee
there
Was
her
husBAND.
AND
his
eye
POP
When
She

toLD
him
what
BaBY
Was
Comeing.

(Douglas) p5

me
Mother
by Eddie

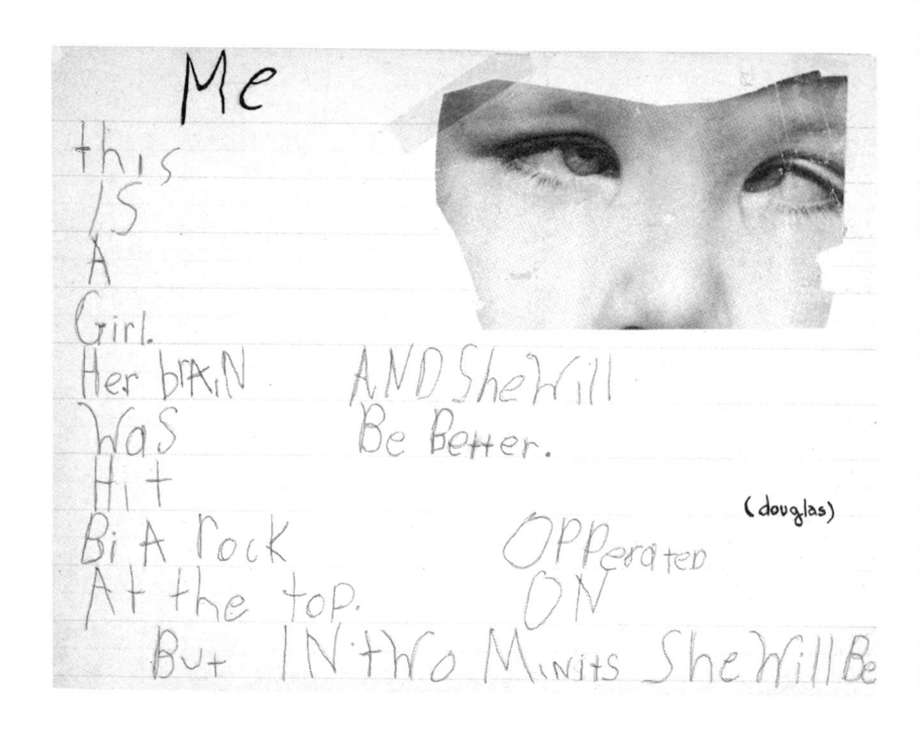
Me
this
IS
A
Girl.
Her brAiN
WaS
Hit
Bi A rock
At the top.
But IN two Minits She Will Be
OPPerated
ON
AND She Will
Be Better.
(douglas)

DaDDy
he
IS
Down
here
all
Waaa
aaa
DOO
BaBy
Kingtut
(Jonathan)

# CHAPTER 8

One Monday, toward the end of October, Miss Silverstein came to our room to invite the class to participate in the school's annual Halloween party, including the traditional costume parade around the school grounds. Many mothers came to photograph this colorful event. Privately, she told me that any disruption by the Transitional Class would only increase the resentment of some parents toward our being in "their" school.

Everyone but Jonathan responded enthusiastically.

"I'll be a ghost," said Kevin.

Eddie was really excited. "I'm going to wrap up in hundreds of bandages and be a mummy."

"That figures," said Douglas. "You're already a mommy's boy!" Eddie was ready to fight, but Douglas disarmed him with a smile and continued. "No, no kiddin', I'll probably wear an astronaut's suit, with oxygen and all."

"Even with the simplest costume, it will be a special day for all of us," Miss Silverstein smiled. "Such an exciting day that we'll have to keep reminding ourselves to obey the rules. And Jonathan, we haven't heard from you."

"Pow, pow! Squish, squish, bang!"

"Yes, I hear your noises, but I want to know what you might wear to our Halloween party," the principal said.

Jonathan seemed to be considering this, then replied, "Have you ever seen people cleaning out a cesspool? I love to step on the b.m. Squish, squish."

At home, Halloween fever was running high. Richie, like Douglas, chose to be an astronaut. For days he argued that I was unreasonable not to let him wear Billy's fishbowl on his head "just for one night." We compromised on spraying his football helmet silver.

Billy would be a cowboy and Ellen a cat. Ann had a problem —too old, she thought, to wear a disguise, too young to consider staying home. "Alecia and I will collect for UNICEF. Then if anybody wants to give up a treat—well—okay."

While I sewed Ellen's costume, the kids made popcorn balls. Though I knew I'd be wiping up syrup for days, it was a pleasure to hear them talking and laughing together. Since Ann had begun the difficult transition into adolescence, she was often disparaging of the others. Family arguments frequently ended with her calling someone a baby.

Before they went to bed, the children brought the trays of popcorn balls into the dining room where I was sewing. I admired their confections.

"Countdown's on," Richie said, kissing me goodnight. "Just three more days."

The waiting was hard at school too. Everyone was high and giggly in anticipation of Friday's Halloween party. Everyone but Douglas. He became surlier by the hour. Work had its settling effect on the others, but he even refused to participate in the phonics game he'd invariably won in the past.

"Come on, Doug," I coaxed. "You can think of a word that begins with str—"

"Haven't I told you before?' he snapped. "Will you turn off the water hoses? Don't pretend you like Africans." He ignored our game until everyone was stumped for a word beginning with X.

"Exile!" he yelled. "Like me," he whispered.

At noon on Thursday I found his note face up at the top of the wastebasket.

Because Doug's grandmother had no phone, I asked the bus

**CENTRAL SCHOOL**

Mrs Craig

---

I would like to see you after school

Doug
Miller

P.S. Your not listening

driver to stop at their apartment and let her know that I would drive Doug home in an hour or two.

After the other boys left, I said, "I found your note, Doug. Won't you tell me, please, what is it I haven't been listening to?"

His depression turned to rage. He ripped all the charts and pictures from the wall, threw chalk, erasers, books in all directions. Then he ran into the closet, his back to me, and began to yell.

"Trying to get me in trouble, huh? You want me to steal some dumb costume? Think my grandmother's got money to spend on some junky thing to make *you* happy?" His voice faltered. He was crying.

"You're the only one who could do it, Doug. Make a costume better than any store has. Use anything you want in the closets. I'll help you."

Within an hour he had transformed a paper bag into a lion's head, with a mane of yellow yarn and plastic straws for whiskers. He also picked up everything he had thrown around, even tacked the charts back on the walls. On the way home we stopped at MacDonald's for hamburgers and french fries. His housing development was more depressing than I had realized. "Douglas," I said as we drove in, "see how much better everything was when you finally told me what was on your mind, instead of bottling it all up inside."

"Look," he opened the car door, "just sympathize, don't criticize." And he was gone.

Halloween at Central School was a great success, due in large measure to the skill of the parade marshal, a perfect replica of Charlie Chaplin. We didn't find out for days that it was Miss Silverstein.

Ceil came to watch the festivities. We noted happily that our class was indistinguishable from the others.

The party was barely over when the Volkswagen bus arrived, so Douglas the Lion, Eddie as Captain Hook, Kevin as an all-too-pretty girl, and Jonathan the Dragon, rode home in costume.

"What a busload!" we laughed as we waved them off.

"How about party time for us?" Ceil suggested. "We don't have to have our conference in this building. We can both get home quickly from that Italian place. What do you say?"

"Sounds great. I just have to get my planbook. Be right out." Doug's note was on my book.

"Look, Ceil. Read this. It's the most eloquent thank-you I've ever received."

We drove separately to Danny's and chose a table in the rear away from the noisy bar, already lined with weekend head-starters.

"It's Friday and after hours at that," Ceil winked, "let's live a little."

"Right."

"A bloody mary and a sausage grinder."

"The same."

She leaned forward. "The kids did so well today, but before we discuss them, tell me about Bill and the family."

We never did get back to the class. We shared concerns about our families and the common problems we faced as working wives and mothers. The daily hassles of rides for the children, shopping, laundry, the inevitable guilty conscience at the end of each day, because something was always left undone. Nothing was resolved, but our professional relationship was deepening into friendship.

That night, the kids were so excited they hardly touched their dinners. When Bill finally excused them from the table, Richie, Billy and Ellen raced upstairs to change into their costumes. Ann grabbed her coat, her UNICEF can and the front door knob all in the same motion.

Our bell rang constantly. When I opened the door at eight, I was shocked to see Ellen and Robin standing there sobbing. After a few minutes, they were calm enough to explain that a neighborhood boy had knocked them down and grabbed their bags. They lost all of their candy, and Robin's glasses fell off and were broken.

Dear mrs craig

the mask work
fine and I had
a good time

Douglas M

Robin began to cry again, but stopped abruptly when Billy came in. Both girls tensed, probably expecting to be ridiculed for not defending themselves in a "two-against-one." Hearing the story, however, Billy was on the phone immediately.

"Mrs. Andrews, this is William Craig. I just want you to know what your son did to my sister and her friend. . . ."

Nothing could have pleased the girls more, unless it was that he then shared his candy with them.

# CHAPTER 9

I watched the boys climbing out of the bus Monday morning. Kevin was missing. Our first absence.

On Tuesday his mother called to say he had tonsillitis and might be out all week. Isolation was too much for Douglas. He moved his desk nearer Eddie's. The day passed without a fight.

By Wednesday, Doug and Eddie were buddies. Doug whispered "Ed, don't tell Kevin we're friends, okay? He'd get all steamed up."

Jonathan was left out, but he had more urgent problems. "Do you know what day it is?" he asked when I called him for reading.

"November fourth?"

"Uh-uh," he replied. It's poop day."

It was.

"I'm sorry you're not ready to stay here today, Jonathan. Miss Silverstein is calling your mother. She'll take you home soon. I hope that tomorrow you'll be able to stay all day."

His mother was close to tears when she led him out. "Squish, squish. Hi, Mom! Poop, poop."

Douglas shook his head. He looked bewildered. "Man, when that kid was born, he musta been an accident. They say God never makes a mistake, but he sure has accidents."

After lunch, he and Eddie painted together, one on either side of the easel. They became confidants.

"Did I ever tell you, Ed, how to steal stuff from Woolworth's?" Douglas was outlining a nude woman.

"No, how?"

"Easy. Just act like you're the manager's son. Walk up and down the aisles like he's your father. Then nobody will watch, so you can drop stuff down your coat."

"That's boss."

"Yeah but don't take it home, see? Leave it under some of the empty boxes behind the store. Then when you want to, you can go and look at it."

"Mmmm," Eddie stepped back to admire his striped paper. "I'll have to show this rainbow to my mother. She thinks I'm crummy, but I'm not. I'm good."

Douglas glanced over. "That looks cool, man. Have you got a pretty mother?"

"Well, in the morning she's all mussed up, but when she puts on that spray for hard-to-manage hair she looks better."

They laughed condescendingly.

"My mother, too," Doug said wistfully.

"You don't even have a mother. The bus driver said that's your grandmother. I saw her today when we picked you up. I hate her because she's colored."

"Do you think that's my grandmother? Heck, that's the cleaning lady." Douglas looked uncomfortable.

"Oh yeah?" Eddie's voice became shrill. "You boog! You're colored too!" Eddie pointed his brush at Douglas.

"Do you think I'm colored?" Douglas kept painting. "See, my mother was married to a colored man for a little while, but he was just my cousin, not my real father. My real father's dead."

"Liar! Liar!" Eddie screamed. "You're going down to the devil!"

Douglas painted a green stripe from Eddie's forehead to his waist. Eddie reciprocated with purple.

"The brushes are for the paper!" I moved in and, caught in the middle, was thoroughly decorated by both artists.

When their brushes were finally dry, and the boys were too spent to continue, I tried cleaning all three of us with a damp sponge. The sponge smeared the paint.

Douglas contemplated his ruined jeans. "By the time my grandmother sees these pants, Mrs. Craig, you better be seeing your travel agent."

No time for the travel agent. Ceil and I had an appointment with Eddie's mother. I spent fifteen minutes in the washroom scrubbing my face and clothes. Then, feeling uncomfortably damp, I waited almost an hour with Ceil before Mrs. Conte sauntered in. She wore a black vinyl mini-coat, spiked heels, and elaborate green eye makeup. "My girl friend was late. She's taking care of the kids."

"We're glad you came," Ceil responded.

We sat in the deserted teachers' lounge, confronting one another on high-backed wooden chairs.

"We've been concerned," Ceil began, "about Eddie's frequent upsets."

Mrs. Conte looked disgusted. Her manicured hand reached for the ashtray. "He's upset! I try to tell that kid how I feel, but he only thinks of himself." Her eyes narrowed suspiciously. "What does he say?"

Ceil deferred to me. "Eddie's worried about all of you, Mrs. Conte. He seems frightened."

"What's he got to be frightened about? His father hits me, not him. Seven years of this misery. My husband turns me off and on like I'm a TV."

"Whether he gets hit or not," Ceil replied, "the situation is very threatening. He sees his father out of control."

"I wouldn't take it from him if I had anyplace to go. He started again last night, but I threw hot coffee at him, and he left."

"He's gone, then?"

She waved her cigarette. "He's always leaving. I can't get rid of him. I wish he'd leave for good. I wish he was dead with his head cut off."

After a moment's pause, Ceil asked, "Have you and your husband considered seeing someone about these problems?"

"Ha! He wouldn't talk to anyone. He never even talks to me. He's so full of hate."

"Why do you think he feels that way, Mrs. Conte?" Ceil asked.

"Listen, he just hates everyone, that's all—me, the kids, his mother. He hated his mother for drinking herself to death, but he's no better." She took a long drag on her cigarette, then spoke more gently. "I could hate too. I could hate my mother for dying when I was born. Why'd she have to have me if she was gonna leave me? I could hate my grandmother too, for putting me in a foster home, but would that do any good?"

"You've had a difficult time, too," Ceil sympathized. "Surely you understand how the fighting affects Eddie. It's impossible for him to settle down here."

"I'll settle him down for you as soon as I get home. Last time I had to beat that kid, he couldn't sit down for three days."

"Please, Mrs. Conte." I found myself pleading, "that's the opposite of what he needs. Let's work together to help Eddie as much as possible. He needs your love and reassurance more than ever."

"Yeah?" She rose, smoothing her sweater into her belt. "Who's going to love me?"

On Thursday morning, Eddie bolted into the room, gasping, "Help! Doug's gonna kill me!" Jonathan, behind him, ducked into the closet and crouched under my coat.

Douglas swaggering in grinning down at the gleaming object projecting from his pocket. It was a paring knife. "Don't worry, Ed, just be a good kid, if you know how. Any more talk about colored people and I'll take care of you. I'll get a switchblade next."

"Let's have it now, Doug." I put out my hand, concentrating on keeping it steady. "You're giving Eddie exactly what he wants."

He stood still. He was listening. "You're letting him get you in trouble. I won't allow him to do this to you. Let me have the knife."

Douglas drew the weapon from his pocket and studied it. Eddie watched suspiciously. Douglas stared at him, then at me. Our eyes met for several seconds. Suddenly dispirited, he shuffled across the room and gently lay the knife in my palm.

"That's a good decision, Doug. You're not letting Eddie get you in trouble."

Eddie, no longer threatened, pranced around his desk. "You're a dirty black-faced nigger," he squealed, "and so's your grandmother."

Douglas looked totally betrayed. He turned toward me. With venom he spat out, "I've got a faggot for a teacher."

I approached Eddie cautiously, clutched his bony shoulder and forced him into his chair. "Jonathan! Douglas! To your seats immediately! We're going to settle this right now! Eddie don't you realize there's a name for everybody, if people are foolish enough to do name-calling?"

He came up with several for me. "Bitch! Whore! Take your crummy hand off my shoulder!"

"I will when you control yourself. Right now you need my help. I'm giving you a paper. You too, Jonathan and Douglas. I don't understand why we have so many fights. I want you to write down what it is you don't like about each other. If you can't do it in words, draw a picture. Begin right away. It must be done before you get your folders."

I slapped a paper on each desk. Jonathan, as usual, drew his ghost family. But for the other two, I had invited a marathon of mutual disparagement. They drew feverishly, in silence, for five minutes.

Douglas held up his picture. "Look at this little pig-eyed face. Freckles all over him. He calls me black, but he's spotted, that's worse! His father musta been a leopard."

Eddie's portrait of Douglas was featureless, just a lopsided brown circle he was furiously coloring in. "Look at this chocolate face. He musta been dipped in Cocoa Marsh. Look at the Cocoa Marsh kid!"

Eddie's imagery amused his intended victim. "How about you? Were you dipped in marshmallow fluff?"

Eddie's tense face broke into a smile.

"Hey, Eddie," Douglas continued, "wanna play connect-the-dots with your freckles? You get first move."

As the freckles on the drawing were connected, a friendship was formed.

"Okay lady, let's have our folders now. Me and my pal don't wanna be having lunch at one o'clock. We wanna have some time for fun. Right, ole buddy?"

# CHAPTER 10

Looking thinner and more pale, Kevin returned the next day. When Douglas ignored him and sat down beside Eddie, Kevin remained in the corner, often turning to look sadly toward Douglas.

Douglas and Eddie worked diligently, encouraging each other to hurry so they would have time to play.

Jonathan still burped and drilled holes in his papers but hadn't soiled since he had been sent home. Moreover, he had begun to make sudden and dramatic progress in reading. At first he had been unable to sound out the simplest words. Now he read fluently at first grade level.

When Jonathan finished, it was Kevin's turn. Walking over to the table, he deliberately bumped into Douglas' desk.

"Hey," Douglas roared, "are you blind?"

Kevin answered in a quiet monotone. "I'm going to tell my mother that you're not ever coming over."

"Why Kev," said Douglas, "I didn't mean no harm to you! It's not that I don't like you or nothing, I just have to intend to my work, but I'm still your faithful companion, remember? You said I was coming over soon."

Kevin slumped into the chair beside me, then drooped forward onto the table. His eyes were shut.

"What's wrong, Kevin?" I put my arm around his shoulder.

No answer.

"Do you feel all right?"

Silence.

"We missed you this week. Is it hard to get back to school?"

"My mother," he murmured.

"Your mother?"

"My mother. She doesn't believe me when I say I'm sick."

"Are you sick now?"

"Mmm . . . sick."

"Where don't you feel well, Kevin?"

"Sick, mmm." His words were barely audible. "I'm homesick, that's what. She doesn't believe me."

I patted his back. "It's hard to come to school when you've been absent."

Suddenly he leaped up, darted into the closet, and closed the door on himself.

Douglas became alarmed. "Listen Kevin, we were having a good morning till you started messing up."

Kevin stuck his head out, then began to pull the door shut on his neck.

"Don't, don't!" Douglas yelled. "You're going to hurt yourself!"

"So what," Kevin answered flatly. "I want to."

"Make him stop, Mrs. Craig," Douglas pleaded. "He's wiping his sweat on us!"

Jonathan bounced in his chair. "Whooeee, he's blowin' his top! He's gonna blast off!"

Kevin's face was scarlet from the pressure on his neck. I rushed to the closet and yanked the door from his grasp. He crumpled to the floor, gasping. Douglas began to whimper.

Eddie, scornful of Douglas' concern, mocked, "You worried about that tomato face? That crazy tomato face is your friend?"

"See what you've done?" Douglas sobbed. "You bum!" He bolted across the room. "You've embarrassed me! Eddie thinks I've got nutty friends. He thinks I taught you to be nuts!" He kicked Kevin in the stomach.

Kevin doubled up in pain, while Douglas went on his all-time rampage. Picking up a chair, he hurled it across the room. Two legs flew off as it cracked a section of blackboard. Coats and jackets were hurled out the window, followed by the wastebasket, papers, and workbooks. I tried to reach him, both physically and with words. He was grunting and snarling, upsetting desks and chairs, scattering papers everywhere.

He grabbed a new tin of chalk from the closet and dumped it, sawdust and all, on Kevin, yelling, "I don't care if you get hurt! I don't care if you die!"

The chalk bounced off Kevin's motionless body. Sawdust filtered into his hair, his eyes and mouth. He gagged and spat.

I caught Douglas' wrist, but he kicked my ankle and ran, calling back, "Shut up, shut up, shut up. . . ." I pursued him to the door and watched him zigzag down the hall, ripping everything off the bulletin boards on both sides as he ran.

Luckily an intercom had just been installed. Miss Silverstein's secretary answered sweetly.

"Doris quick! Tell Miss Silverstein that Douglas is somewhere in the building, and we need the nurse immediately for Kevin."

"Hmm? Really? My gosh. Oh, okay."

Seconds later, Miss Silverstein and Mrs. Rogers, the nurse, rushed in, visibly distressed by the havoc in the hall. Our room looked like the aftermath of a tornado.

Kevin had recovered enough to howl. Eddie was prancing around, holding the broken chair aloft. "That boog did it! He broke school property. Now who's a punk?"

Jonathan, having taken cover under his desk, was grunting suspiciously. He zapped the nurse and principal with his invisible atomic gun. "Pow—bam—got ya—you're dead!"

Mrs. Rogers went to Kevin. Eyeing me accusingly, she demanded, "What happened to him?"

"Douglas kicked him in the stomach."

"My God! He could have a rupture!" The nurse, in her late forties, was a tall, heavy-set woman, capable but formidable. Effortlessly, she scooped up the limp child. Chalk and sawdust rained from both of them. "This whole setup just babies kids, lets them get away with murder. In a bigger class they wouldn't dare behave this way. Four kids in a room, a waste of time and money! Just spoiling them, that's what I say."

Her words came with such vehemence that I realized she had felt this way from the beginning. I thought of the innocent classmates these children had victimized previously, but it was no time to justify the program.

She stormed out, Kevin draped limply in her arms.

"Hey, Miss Silverstein," Eddie was gleeful, "is Doug's grandmother gonna hafta pay? My mother says they're on welfare. Will he go to jail?"

I eased the chair from Eddie's clutch. "You gonna call the police, Mrs. Craig? Are they gonna arrest that nigger?"

Miss Silverstein tugged at Jonathan. She sniffed, then shot me a look confirming the worst. But the morning had already been so disastrous, I decided that I might as well let Jonathan stay this time.

I put his and Eddie's lunchboxes on their desks. Once again food proved a panacea. I set up the record player, and Eddie chose the Peter Pan album. Music enhanced the calm.

Miss Silverstein and I whispered in the doorway. I tried to describe the sequence of events. She smiled knowingly. "You don't have to tell me how these kids can explode. I've been in the business too long. Let's just hope Kevin is okay. Mr. Jakowsky and I will look around for Douglas."

I began to straighten up the room, hiding the broken furniture so as not to remind ourselves of our failings. Jonathan and Eddie were still lost in the land of Tinkerbell and Peter Pan.

The intercom buzzed. Mrs. Roger's voice. "Kevin wasn't hurt, just upset. Send his coat and lunchbox to my office right away. His mother is coming now."

"I will. And thanks. Will you tell Kevin I hope he feels better?" She clicked off.

Just as I was about to call the office to have Mr. Jakowsky retrieve Kevin's coat from the playground, he came limping in, loaded with everything Douglas had ejected.

"Mr. Jakowsky, you're a mind reader! Here, let me help you."

He was limping more than usual. "Been chasing that boy of yours, when I saw these things out there. He's in the teachers' parking lot, jumping from one car to another. No sense me following him, he just moves faster than I do."

Douglas hadn't shown up when the bus drove in at one o'clock. After sending Jonathan and Eddie out, I ran to the faculty parking lot, hoping to spot Douglas in time. I envisioned the nightmare of driving over to tell his grandmother we couldn't find him. Frantic, I raced to beg the bus driver to wait a few minutes, but he was already pulling away. As the bus turned onto the road, Douglas' face suddenly appeared in the rear window. He saw me, grinned, and raised his fingers in the peace sign.

"Can't bear to let them go, eh?" Ceil had driven in while I stood numbly watching the bus depart. "Where's your coat, Mrs. Craig?" She leaned out the car window. "Haven't you noticed, it's beginning to snow? You know, November. Hey, hustle it! Did you forget the meeting? Get your coat. I'm driving you over."

She clucked sympathetically as I recounted the day right through the finale with Douglas and his peace sign. "No wonder you looked so catatonic!" She giggled. It was infectious. In minutes we were walking into the Administration Building, wiping away tears of mirth.

The meeting had been called to discuss the intake of two new pupils, this time girls. It was hard to concentrate as Sandra's case was being presented. Today's drama kept replaying in my head.

"What do you think?" Jim Hanley was addressing me. "Does Sandra sound like a good candidate to you?"

Why hadn't I listened? But wouldn't any girl be easier than another boy? "Well, I'd like to hear about the other girl before we decide. It's important, isn't it, that they be compatible?"

Claire Megan, the social worker who was making the referral, presented Julie's case. "I have been seeing the Neumayers regularly since the beginning of the year. They're an older couple. She's forty-seven and he's forty-nine. For many years they had considered adopting, but Mr. Neumayer was a master sergeant in the Army and because of frequent relocations they never followed through at any agency. Finally, just before his discharge seven years ago they were stationed near Philadelphia and heard about the Pearl Buck agency. As you know, it deals almost exclusively with difficult-to-place children and often with couples who have been unable to adopt elsewhere.

Julie's unwed mother had kept her until she was two, making it more difficult to place her. In the next twelve months she lived in three different foster homes. Each foster mother complained about the child's tantrums and frequent nightmares. Within a month after they applied, the Neumayers were given custody of Julie and had moved here. Mr. Neumayer entered a training program at the electronics plant. They had problems with the three-year-old from the beginning."

"That makes me wonder," Ceil interrupted, "do we know why Julie's mother finally gave her up? At first, she obviously intended to raise her. Did she change her mind because she found the child so difficult?"

Claire replied, "I was curious about that too. I tried to pursue it. but the records are inadequate. They state simply that the mother could no longer keep her. The test results may answer some questions. When the Neumayers first took Julie to a pediatrician, he advised them that the child was functionally retarded but attributed this to her deprivation. He predicted that with love and stimulation her mental development would accelerate. Mrs. Neumayer says she knew then the adoption was a mistake and wanted to return the child, but her husband would not agree.

"Julie was referred for social work service in kindergarten, two years ago. She was a nervous, whiny child, with many psychosomatic complaints. Now, in second grade, she spends most mornings in the nurse's office, and becomes hysterical at the suggestion that she return to class. Even with individual attention, her work is poor. She has no friends; the kids all tease her."

The social worker looked up from her notes.

"At this point we aren't even sure of the depth of pathology. Are we dealing with a painfully unhappy, mismanaged girl, or one who is seriously disturbed? We feel her placement in this class will serve a diagnostic purpose."

"Julie is one of the few children we've screened who's still in school," Mr. Hanley observed. "How do her parents feel about Transitional Class?"

"Mrs. Neumayer is not happy," Claire replied. "I saw her last week. She talked at length about how Julie deliberately provokes by bedwetting, among other things. She wants her sent 'someplace where they handle that kind of child.' She will go along with our recommendation only because she hopes it will lead to residential placement."

"Jeez," Mr. Hanley said to himself. Then aloud, "Miss Wood, you did the testing?"

She nodded. "Psychologicals reveal high average ability, but feelings of deep depression and insecurity with inadequate defenses. There was a possibility of minimal cerebral dysfunction, and since the exact extent was unknown we asked for an EEG and skull X-rays. Both were negative. The neurologist concluded that although there is a visual motor lag, it is probably maturational in nature."

"One thing we can do for Julie right away," Ceil said, "is to have her seen by Dr. Bialek at the clinic. If he could put her on Tofranil for the bed-wetting it would be one break in the vicious circle."

The committee voted unanimously to accept both girls. We agreed they would enter Transitional Class in one week.

On the following Thursday, Ceil called after school to say the plans had been upset. "Sandra's father has been transferred. They'll be leaving in two weeks. There's no sense starting with her, of course, yet I don't think we should postpone Julie's arrival. We'll be looking for another girl. It's far from ideal to have only one, but I don't see that we have much choice."

While I was on the phone with Ceil, the storm that had threatened all day broke full force. By the time I got home I was completely drenched.

The children had been soaked too and were sitting in the living room in bathrobes and slippers watching TV. I changed my clothes and started supper, but just as I slid the meat loaf into the oven, the electricity suddenly went out.

Richie propped his transistor on the kitchen counter. We heard that because a major trunk line had been severed, power would not be restored in our area for several hours. Searching the refrigerator while Ann held up a flashlight, I came up with a package of hot dogs. Bill brought in our biggest logs from the garage and piled them in the living room fireplace. The kids roasted the hot dogs on fondue forks and marveled at how "neat" it must have been in "the old days" when people cooked all their meals in the fireplace. They even suggested that we try it for a week.

By morning the power had been restored, but the kids were still animated and chatted incessantly about last night's fun. Ann was especially pleased to have such an ironclad excuse for not doing her homework. "I can't possibly get in trouble, can I, Mom?"

But what had been exciting for my own children had been traumatizing for others.

Kevin came to school subdued and depressed. Eddie raced around frantically. "Someone turned off the goddamn lights! We just got crackers for supper!"

My explanation of the storm's havoc angered Douglas. Holding his jacket as if it were a bat, he pounded it repeatedly against the wall. "So that's what did it!" he snarled. "My grandmother said we didn't have no money for the lights!"

Jonathan, who at best had difficulty separating fantasy from reality, was most deeply affected. "All night," he cried, "rats and monsters came down from the attic! I had to climb to the roof for safety. Then I saw a plane crash because of the dark. It burned and burned. I got my flashlight to signal the other pilots, but their planes crashed too."

We talked at length, did finger paintings, and played records, but none of these activities soothed Jonathan.

"Oh, oh," he moaned at bus time, putting on his coat. "I hope there won't be more rats and monsters tonight!"

# CHAPTER 11

Mrs. Neumayer and Julie were waiting at school when I arrived Monday morning. The mother, a thin tense-faced woman, had a parting message for both Julie and me.

"Mrs. Craig, I will expect a progress report on this child every Friday."

"Julie," her voice was cold, "you are to cooperate. We've done all we can for you. Now it's your turn."

She was an adorable girl, small and chunky, with dimpled hands and knees. Her round, petulant face had a light sprinkle of freckles across the bridge of her nose. Her eyes were big and blue, and her auburn hair, which was very long, was now in pigtails with ribbons on the ends. After her mother left, she sat sucking her thumb. I tried to put her at ease and asked her to choose a cubby. She only whispered, "this one" without removing her thumb from her mouth.

The bus came. It was apparent that last week's words regarding Julie's imminent entry were lost in postblackout excitement. The boys were stunned to have a girl in the class. They devised circuitous routes to their desks to avoid approaching her. Instead of the usual protests, they accepted their folders almost gratefully and buried themselves in their assignments. On the surface, this was our most successful day, but there was too unnatural a calm. Heads turned periodically for surreptitious glances at the frightened girl.

The "honeymoon" period of model behavior often exhibited by a new pupil now extended to the whole class and lasted an entire week.

By Friday, Douglas was becoming coolly objective. "She's a good-looking girl," he observed during his reading period. At noon, Eddie, en route to the boys' bathroom, remarked to Douglas, "Some day I'm gonna see that girl's pisser." They both laughed. For the full week, Jonathan managed to curb his disruptive outbursts. He was more aware of Julie's presence than he had previously been of all the others.

But Kevin's reaction was the most unexpected. Small gestures revealed his enormous interest—he would move his coat closer to hers, or time getting in line so that she would be next to him.

The next school week was a short one, just three days before Thanksgiving. In that brief time the veneer and gallantry wore thin. Julie had episodes of weeping, then fanatically turning on herself, biting her arms and hands. I learned to subdue her, holding my arms around her until she was calm. This depressed the boys. Jonathan returned to whistling and grunting, Eddie and Douglas to their ambivalent relationship—unprovoked warfare, sudden reconciliations.

Kevin, most distressed by Julie's behavior, tapped his feet and accomplished nothing at all, justifying himself frequently. "I can't work with that freckle-faced Julie making so much noise."

Thanksgiving became a focal point for all activities. The children used Indian symbols in their creative writing. Art projects evolved from brilliantly painted headdresses to the life-sized canoe Douglas and Eddie created by cutting and stapling giant sheets of oak tag.

With props completed, we agreed to share lunches the day before the holiday. The children all chose to be Indians. I was the lone Pilgrim. Jonathan brought in his flashlight. "See? This is the original one I used to signal the planes. I covered it with red cellophane this morning, so it would look like our fire."

Inspired by Jonathan's contribution, Douglas and Kevin tugged in a tumbling mat from the gym. "This will be our campsite, okay? Jonathan, you put your flashlight in the middle," Douglas directed.

Eddie, with neither permission nor explanation, bolted from the room, but returned in minutes, his arms full of twigs, which he skillfully arranged around the flashlight. He and Douglas lowered all the shades. The result was pure magic, a glowing campfire.

When had they changed? I wondered. When had they begun trying to get along with one another?

There was a last practicality, washing up before lunch. The mood was broken by Julie's screams. I found her in the bathroom, Douglas' arm around her neck. He and Kevin were lifting up her skirt.

"Douglas! Kevin! How dare you do this to her!" I was furious. "Get out of here immediately!"

Kevin was mortified at being caught. Douglas was angered by the interruption. "Just button up your lip, lady, and keep your mind out of men's business."

"It is my business to see that you don't take advantage of people, either of you. And protecting Julie is my business. Don't you dare do anything like this again!"

The possible consequences were flashing through my mind. Should I report them immediately to Miss Silverstein? Should they be sent home now? Or might it still be possible to salvage any part of the Thanksgiving celebration, which had seemed so significant in view of their progress just minutes ago.

Julie's expression, frightened but somehow pleased with the attention, encouraged me to try.

"I'd like to return to our room now. I'd like to forget this incident and start again. Would you?"

Kevin gulped. His face was scarlet. Douglas' bravado vanished. He nodded as the first tear rolled into his mouth.

We sat cross-legged on the mat around the rosy "fire"—Douglas and Kevin, two subdued Indians; Julie, surprisingly complacent; Jonathan and Eddie rendering bloodcurdling war cries.

The clay peace pipe Eddie had molded passed hands solemnly.

I was relieved to have made this decision. I felt sure that they would return from vacation remembering this rewarding experience.

"May we please wear our headdresses on the bus?" Douglas asked respectfully.

"And I get to take the canoe," Eddie added.

"You gotta be kidding," Douglas challenged. "I did more work than you."

"Oh yeah? I stapled the whole damn thing!" Eddie screamed.

"See you later, little punk." Douglas lifted the canoe onto his back, arching the bow over his shoulder.

"Let's be fair," I said. "We'll draw lots and see who wins."

But Eddie lunged at the middle of the canoe, momentarily wresting it from Douglas' grasp. Douglas pulled. Eddie fell back against the wall, sprang forward, and tugged so ferociously that Douglas was dragged halfway across the room before the oak tag tore.

The Indians filed out. Douglas and Eddie went home triumphantly, each with a jagged section of canoe draped on his shoulder.

On Wednesday night my parents flew in from Boston, as they did every Thanksgiving. Bill and the boys met them at the airport. I looked forward to their visits for weeks, sharing the children's excitement. We saw them so infrequently that every minute of the holiday was special, and everything we did—hiking in the woods behind our house, choosing pumpkins, playing games—was more fun for having them with us. Besides, it was the only time we had really good pumpkin pie, and I had never been able to duplicate my mother's turkey dressing.

This year our Thanksgiving dinner was particularly memorable. We had invited our close friend, Brendan Donohoe, a local waiter with the soul of an Irish poet. He and my father were a perfect complement. They held us all spellbound for hours with their tales of Tipperary and County Cork.

But when Brendan was gone and the children were asleep, my parents expressed concern for our future. Hadn't Bill been rash to quit his job, with our house not nearly paid off and four children to send to college? What if his book weren't well received?

We sat up until three, reassuring them that we had done the right thing, and that the book would be a success. Yet they had touched on the uncertainties that troubled Bill and me most, and long after I had gone to bed, I could hear Bill pacing in the livingroom.

# CHAPTER 12

It was December tenth, but somehow I wrote ninth on the board. Eddie noticed immediately.

"You're stupid, you know that? I don't really mean it, but you're funny." This was the closest he'd come to a friendly remark or to any revision of an insulting one.

Douglas testified in my defense. "Mrs. Craig's way smarter than you, Eddie. She's gone through experiences you've never dreamed of." I nodded knowingly.

Eddie was taking great care tucking new beige gloves into his coat pocket. Until then he'd come bare-handed despite the cold.

The routine of folders and individual help was now well established, not that the incentive was pride in accomplishment. The goal still was to eat lunch on time.

"Kevin is first today," I called. As usual, I waited for him to find his book, a pencil, and this time a handkerchief from his coat. Then came his maddening shuffle by way of each desk, as he checked what the others were doing.

"We have a new step in adding today, Kevin. Let me show you."

"I already know," he said peevishly.

"Not how to carry, Kevin, look." He turned his back to me and stared at the ceiling.

"Okay, do it." It was difficult to keep the irritation from my voice.

In ten minutes he slid the paper across the table, every example wrong. "Can you see now," I asked, "why it's better to start with the explanation?"

"So what if they're all wrong? What else do I have to do?"

"This again, only correctly. I'll explain it to you now, but you'll have to do the work at home after school."

"Uh-uh. My mother's taking me somewhere tonight. I can't."

"That's okay, then. Just have your mother write a note saying you were too busy for homework." Scowling, he yanked the paper from my hand and stuffed it in his shirt pocket.

Later, as Julie scurried by him to come to read, Kevin edged his foot in her path. She tripped and cried.

"I saw that, Kevin!" Eddie piped. "You did that on purpose."

"I did not," he lied. "I ought to know. I know more than you. Don't forget I was in first grade twice."

Julie recovered quickly and evened the score by confiding to me in a stage whisper, "Kevin thinks he's cute, but he isn't. I only like cute boys. That's how girls are."

Kevin heard, and reacted by biting off each corner of his folder, then chewing the pieces. He slumped forward dramatically as if poisoned.

Even worse, Julie ignored him.

"Don't ask me to do any work today." Julie held the back of her hand to her forehead. "I'm not feeling well. I throw up if I have to do too much."

"It won't be too much for you, Julie." She sucked her thumb as we looked at her paper, smudged black where she had rubbed errors by spitting on her finger.

"I'm messy, aren't I? Everyone's always looks better. I'm going to throw mine away."

Kevin raised his head. "Do what I used to do at my old school. Put down any answer. I don't care if I get them all wrong!"

"Me too," Julie agreed. "That's what I do."

Kevin's interruption had been intended to irritate her, but instead she had allied herself with him. He couldn't stand it. "I can't work with that freckle-faced girl making so much noise!" he howled.

Douglas put down his pencil. "I can't be your friend, Kevin. I can't be friends with a girl-fighter. Just leave her alone and get your work done. It takes a lot of pride to get things done."

"Mind your own business, big mouth." Kevin was daring today.

"You're going to regret it," Douglas warned.

"Kevin is like me," Julie declared, her hand on her hips. "An instigator. That's a boy or girl who goes around starting trouble. That's what my mother calls me."

"What are you complainin' about, Kevin?" Eddie had been absorbed in his tracing of a skeleton. "You know it's not hard in here. I'm going to stay in this room right through college."

Although I sometimes found myself waiting too long before intervening, I was glad not to have interrupted this dialogue.

Everyone that day had one assignment in common: finding a picture of a mammal and writing a story about it. Jonathan now stared in horror at a German shepherd in *Life* magazine. "Woof, woof. I'm not afraid of dogs like you. Grrrr." But his voice trembled.

"That's a nice picture you found."

"Stay away, back off! My radar's on you! This is an attack dog, stay away!"

"It's a photograph, Jonathan," I persisted.

"Well, I've got my photograph." Douglas sounded belligerent. "And it's the only mammal I can find, so you better be satisfied. It's a dead mammal."

He held up a picture of a TV dinner.

I laughed, and after a few seconds his intimidating scowl broke into a wide grin. Later, when I sat with him, he had something else on his mind. "Look." He cupped a limp dollar in his palm. "Know what I'm gonna get? I'm getting me a Jaguar model. I've got the motor already, but the car was too big to steal, so I got me a dollar."

"Where?"

"From my grandmother," he said defensively. "Listen, don't tell. She'll never suspect me. She doesn't think I have the courage to go in her pocketbook."

"Did you think of asking her first, Doug?"

He slapped his hand to his forehead. "Oh help her, somebody! Is she retarded!"

"If it's so important, let's think of a way that won't be unfair to anyone else."

"Listen, detective, shut up! You're getting into family business!" Then, less harshly, "Hey, you're my friend aren't you?

Can't I tell you something without you turning on the hoses?"

"I'm glad to be your friend, but you don't sound happy about taking that money."

"Oh bull!" He picked up my plastic pen and bore down on it till it snapped in half. "There! Don't think I'm sorry about that either!" He rushed to the door. With a challenging look, he placed his right foot over the threshold.

Please don't go, I begged silently. "Just remember the school rule. Leaving without permission means you're not allowed back the next day."

"Oh, you don't want me here tomorrow? You are sick, sick, sick." He began to spin, repeating "sick, sick, sick." I caught his arm. "Let go, bitch." He bit deeply into my hand, then jumped back in horror at the sight of his toothmarks. The pain was so piercing I turned away, unable to speak.

"I don't like how Douglas talks to you!" Eddie shrilled.

"Just because you're a new punk, don't think you're boss!" Douglas flared back.

"I hate your attitude!" Eddie continued. "I'd like to punch you in the nose!"

Douglas strutted arrogantly. A showdown seemed inevitable, but he stopped at Kevin's side and patted his shoulder. "Let's not come here anymore, pal. I can go over to your house."

Kevin rose and whispered, pointing to me.

They laughed. "Ya! We'll never tell her anything again! She probably expects me to get her another pen. She's been yelling about hers since I broke it."

Kevin looked out the window. His voice was vague. "At home, I break everything of mine. My mother lets me." He paused, as if reflecting on why she wouldn't stop him. "I even broke the model my father made me. Busted the end right off."

Douglas looked puzzled. "Don't you feel sorry later?"

"No, it makes me happy."

My hand felt better. The intense pain had passed. "Douglas, I'll see you in the hall immediately. Everyone else be ready for lunch."

"What now? Now what?" he whined, but followed.

"Doug, I'm sorry. You're not ready to be with us today. You may not hurt people, me or anyone else. If you can't remember, you don't belong here." Consequences had to be tempered with the reality that his grandmother could not be reached by phone. "You'll have to spend the rest of the day in Miss Silverstein's office." He started to run.

"If you go, you can't come back tomorrow either!" He darted into the teachers' lounge, where he began to wail loudly. Frustrated at not being able to leave the others, I got Miss Silverstein on the intercom and briefed her quickly.

"I'll get him," she responded.

The children nibbled their lunches in silence, all monitoring Douglas' sobs, which suddenly turned to screams. Then silence. I tried to move casually toward the hall, but Julie and Eddie were equally curious and joined me at the doorway. We stared as Miss Silverstein ushered a docile Douglas into her office.

Doug's outburst exacted its toll on his classmates. They sat silent and depressed the rest of the afternoon.

When the bus came, Eddie had a tantrum. "My mother's gonna kill me! She'll kill me! Somebody took my gloves!"

Ten frantic minutes later, Julie yelled, "Douglas did it, he's the glove snitcher!" And she withdrew them triumphantly from his desk.

I expected Ceil after school. She was seeing each child weekly, and I was anxious to hear her opinions. She arrived with containers of fresh coffee and a bag of sweet rolls.

"You make me feel better already."

"That's my plan," she laughed. "How's everything going?"

In reconstructing the events I found myself dwelling on Kevin and his maddening, subtle ways of causing trouble.

"He's going to get worse, even harder to manage," she said. "He's beginning to release some of the anger that's been binding him, but he feels too helpless to be really aggressive. He'll take that passive posture and through it try to control those around him. He's suspicious of anyone wanting to help him. He's so afraid of being hurt. Kevin has gone all his life without having his basic dependency needs gratified. We know it's going to be a long haul with him."

We devoured the pastries. Since taking on the Transitional Class, I found myself ravenous at the end of each school day. "Let me tell you about Douglas and Eddie. I think I should be wearing a referee's uniform."

She listened attentively. "Eleanor, when I hear it, something else comes through. Despite what you're saying, the frequency and duration of their upsets seem to have lessened. There are times now when they're actually getting along together."

"Gee, I don't know, Ceil. I really can't see it that way yet, but it's encouraging that you think so."

"Let me tell you about my last session with Eddie," Ceil continued. "He played with the dolls in the dollhouse. The father urinated in the toilet, washed his hair in it, and of course fell in and drowned. While he was being buried, the mother tumbled into the grave on top of him. As he was acting this out, Eddie was able to talk about his fear that his father will come back and that his mother will be unable to protect them. The kid is so full of anxiety it's amazing that he can function at all."

"God, Ceil, I feel ashamed to have ever been impatient with him!"

"No! It would be wrong not to expect anything from him because of his problems. The problems aren't going to disappear. We just want him to cope with them a little better. Incidentally, I've been seeing Jonathan's parents regularly, as you know. I've been worried about him. He's really in another world, but they insist there's nothing wrong with him. They've been so resistant to psychiatric help that I've given them an ultimatum. After this month we won't keep him in the class unless he's in treatment."

"I'm glad to hear it. Let's hope it works."

"I've got to run dear. Everyone okay at home?"

"Fine. Tonight's Ann's fourteenth birthday!"

"How exciting! Tell Ann congratulations. See you next week."

# CHAPTER 13

The next day the children were late. At nine-fifteen there was a startling blast from a horn in the driveway. Then another and another.

The intercom buzzed. "Your bus driver's having a fit. Will you see what's wrong?"

I rushed out. Mr. Dixon's face was purple, apoplectic. Kids were tumbling back and forth over the seats in the compact minibus. Through closed windows I could hear Julie crying and the boys yelling.

Mr. Dixon leaned out. "You get this mob outta here! I never seen such little bastards."

When they spotted me, everyone scrambled for the door to be first with his grievances, except Eddie who was trapped briefly trying to climb through the window. They shoved and fought their way up the stairs into the building.

"You called me witch doctor, Kevin," cried Julie. "I'm telling the teacher."

"You started it, Kevin," Douglas yelled. "I heard you teasing Julie and Jonathan.

"And you hit me hard," Julie added. "Eddie too. He hit me after Kevin did."

Douglas was enraged. "I oughta beat you guys up. Pickin' on a little kid! You know Julie is just a little kid."

We were in the building now. Kevin, quite pleased with the accusations against him, led the way to our room.

Eddie was still hyped up, dancing around Julie and Jonathan, sticking out his tongue, making donkey ears with his hands.

"I say Eddie's the worst," Julie sniffed.

"They're both girl teasers," Douglas charged.

Kevin sat angelically, hands folded on his desk. Douglas had just sat down when Eddie crept up behind him and swung a metal lunchbox at the back of his head. "Duck, Douglas!" I screamed. He missed being hit by a fraction of an inch, only because the lunchbox broke. The container skidded across the floor. Eddie still gripped the handle.

"Okay, here's what you did!" He waved the metal bar in Douglas' face. "You broke my lunchbox! You owe me two dollars!"

"That's ridiculous, Eddie." I said. "You were trying to hurt Douglas with it! It's lucky for you the lunchbox did break. You might have hurt him badly."

"You're protecting him? You're protecting that glove stealer? Nothing's safe with him. I'm getting out of here. I'm leaving my gloves in Miss Silverstein's office all day. *You* can trust that boog thief, I don't." Eddie left without being issued my usual warning about unexcused departures. I desisted, sure that he'd return and not sorry to have him leave.

Remarkably calm, Douglas beckoned me to his desk. In a subdued voice he confided, "I think Eddie's troubled, the way he's been acting."

"You think he tries to hurt people when he's unhappy?"

"Naturally," he nodded.

Eddie danced in. "There! She's keeping my gloves every day. I told her to put them in the safe."

I surveyed the Transitional Class. Eddie was anxious, Douglas stoic, Kevin smug, Julie tearful, and Jonathan tense, about to blow his top.

"No folders today." No smiles, either. "We're invited to the sixth grade Christmas program at ten. Before we go you may write a story or draw a picture of what you would like for Christmas or Hanukkah."

"I'm not drawing a goddamn picture," said Eddie, reaching for the paper.

"I ain't doin' no story," Kevin grumbled.

"Fine. Here's a drawing paper for you too. Jonathan, which do you choose?"

"Stay away! My radar's on you! My rays will get you!"

As I approached, he closed his eyes tightly. "Get away! I'm blurring my vision! The rays are on you!"

"Look, Jonathan, I'm still here. Open your eyes."

He squinted. "Oh no! No! Everything's gone wrong today! Everything! Everyone's picking on me, here and at home too."

"Tell me." I knelt beside him.

He whined, whistled, and burped.

"Tell me in words."

"Y—y—yesterday . . . at . . . home . . . I . . . was . . . m—m—m—making a . . . big hole," he had to force the words, "a big hole in my backyard. These kids came over to watch. I warned them to stay back, stay behind the tree, because my rays are dangerous, but they wouldn't, they wouldn't!" He winced. Even the telling was painful. "They stepped out and laughed at me. I hadda chase them away with my shovel, but my father saw me doing it and he hit me on the bottom. He hit me hard!" He was close to tears.

"Of course you don't like being hit or having kids tease you. But good for you for being able to tell about it. That's hard too. And take another look, Jonathan. Your rays aren't affecting me. They didn't affect the kids yesterday. You don't have dangerous rays."

He looked uncertain but less troubled.

"How do you spell 'wish,' Mrs. Craig?" Julie interrupted.

"How do you thpell with, Mithith Kegg?" Kevin mimicked.

"Why don't you leave her alone, Kevin?" demanded Douglas.

"No, nosy."

Julie took advantage of Douglas' support. "Kevin makes me make mistakes."

"Ha-ha-ha." Kevin mocked her.

"Ha-ha-ha to you, Kevin," Douglas responded.

"Okay, Doug." Kevin knew how to hurt. "You're never coming over. Me and my mother don't like kids like you."

It worked. Douglas was deflated.

A Wish Doug Miller

Oh Oh Oh how I Wish That HaPPiness Shall Come
TO OTher PeoPLe.. Like Eddie Conte.
I Know That HaPPiness Can Come To Eddie if He Could
Try A Little Harder in School.

I Wish I Can Die

Christmas wish

Kevin

y julie Neumayer

If I war a dog.

I will bark and bark all day.

I am a old old dog.

I will die soon.

My famuly will be sad.

*Holiday Wishes*

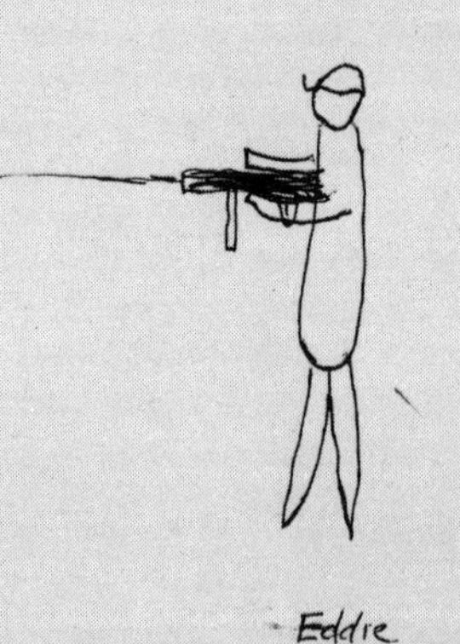

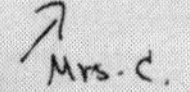


Eddre

(Eddie xmas wish)

"I know what's wrong, Douglas," Julie comforted. "Kevin's jealous. He's used to just having you two. That's why."

"Don't tell me what I am, smarty-farty." Kevin thumbed his nose at her.

Jonathan was in trouble. I was becoming adept at recognizing the warnings. He started with sputtering sounds. I pulled him up firmly, hoping to remove him before the other kids noticed. "Let's go quickly. Into the bathroom."

"I can't help it. Squish, pow. I don't want to get up."

"Of course you can help it. You control your body. I got you up this time, but soon you'll be in charge of yourself."

He left shaking his head, bewildered that I should be so unreasonable.

Jonathan returned, and I collected the papers. I was sure Douglas would have mentioned a model car as his Christmas wish, but he had written a sensitive note wishing happiness to his enemy Eddie. Julie wanted to be a dog, a dead dog, which her family would mourn. Kevin, too, wished himself dead, in a cheery coffin with curtains and a chimney. Jonathan's ghost family scolded baby for wet pants. Eddie sketched me wearing a witch's hat, about to be executed. He was holding the gun.

The other classes were parading past our room into the auditorium for the program.

Checking the "Leaders Chart", devised after countless battles for first place, I read, "Julie is leader today. Douglas next. Then Eddie."

Eddie had other ideas. "I'm not going," he whined. "I'm not leaving this room." His tone was pathetic, as if he were afraid of the unfamiliar auditorium.

"I'll walk with you, Eddie. You and I will be partners." If there were anyone to leave him with, I would not have insisted. "You'll enjoy the program."

He became frantic. He kicked over the easel, luckily free of paint.

"I see how much it means to you, Eddie. If you calm down you may stay in the room. Sit here. I'll take the class to the program and be right back." He sat.

Sally Abbott's group was shuffling along behind us, single file.

"Sally," I turned. "Could you watch my kids a few minutes? I've got a problem."

"Sure."

Eddie had taken the clown punching bag from the closet. He was hurling it across the room.

"That's not waiting quietly, Eddie."

"Who cares? Why should I do anything you say? You don't even know what happened."

He mounted the prone punching bag, straddling it as if riding a horse, then pounded down on it with his fists.

"Something happened?"

"You're so stupid! You don't even know! *He* came home last night. He just came to look for money. I hid under the bed. He put my mother in the closet and tried to find her money, but she got out. She threw the radio at him. When he left, his head was all bloody. If he ever comes again, he's not getting in. I'll put all my strength against the door. I'll tell him, 'Get outta here! Don't ever come back!' " Now standing, he karate-chopped the plastic clown. It reeled back, then rocked toward him, its foolish painted grin mocking his anger. "If you do I'll chop you with a knife. I'll never call you my father again." Sobbing, he draped himself across the inflated punching bag.

"Oh Eddie, I'm sorry. It must be very hard for you."

"Shut up! Shut up! I don't wanna talk about it!"

"Okay, no talk. I'll just sit here with you."

Within five minutes he seemed calm. I was becoming concerned about the others.

"Eddie," I said softly, "I want to tell Miss Abbott to be in charge of our class for the entire program. May I leave you? I'll be right back."

He nodded his head slightly.

I hurried across the hall. It took a minute to spot her in the sea of heads. I tiptoed up. "Sally, would you watch my kids for the whole play and see them back to the room?"

"Okay. Anything serious?"

"Eddie didn't want—" There was a sudden commotion in the back of the room. All heads turned. Someone said, "It's one of those nuts."

Eddie was kicking Miss Silverstein. A male teacher jumped up and grabbed him, pinning his arms behind his back.

"Very serious." I replied.

Mr. Fairman was still holding him when I reached the office. Eddie looked pale. His body shook.

Miss Silverstein beckoned me aside. "He was standing in the doorway exposing himself. I think we removed him before anyone realized."

"Oh, no!"

"I'm excluding him for two days, mostly to let him know he can't kick me. We'll have to talk to Ceil Black about the other problem."

"Right. But I wish we didn't have to send him home. Apparently there's been a big upset there."

Miss Silverstein was sympathetic yet firm. "Mr. Fairman, I'm sure you can let go now. Mrs. Craig would you get Eddie's things? Your mother's going to be coming for you, Eddie."

"No, no! I want to stay here! Don't send me home," he cried.

"We'll talk about it. Come into my office.

I walked out of the office, full of guilt for having left Eddie alone in our room. A little progress, then a big setback. Would it always be this way?

Someone jumped when I entered the room. It was Julie. "You're supposed to be at the Christmas play," I said automatically. For a moment it didn't register that my opened pocketbook was in her hand. She dropped it.

"Julie, what are you doing? What's going on?"

She darted into the closet and buried herself under the coats. I picked up the purse. Nothing was missing. I shoved it back in the desk drawer and sat down, too stunned and depressed to respond to her muffled sobs.

Minutes passed before she spoke. "It's because you . . . you," she cried, "you have everything!"

She ran out of the closet and threw her arms around my neck, pressing her wet face into mine. "I'm sorry, I'm sorry, Mrs. Craig!"

"Oh, Julie, Julie. What do I have that you could want?" I stroked her hair.

"I—" she wept, "I don't have anything!"

"But you do! You're a lovely girl with a pretty face and lots of nice clothes."

"No, no! Nobody likes me. Kevin hates me. I don't have any friends."

The intercom signaled. "We're still waiting for Eddie's things." The secretary sounded annoyed.

"Would you come and get them, please, Doris? I can't bring them right now."

I placed Eddie's coat and broken lunchbox on his desk. "Come on, Julie. Let's both wash our faces in the teachers' room. We look like those Weeping Wanda dolls." She clutched my hand.

After school I began recording the day's events so I could give Ceil a detailed account. But each thought was more disheartening than the last: Jonathan's dangerous rays, the children's tragic Christmas wishes, the bloody head of Eddie's father. Finally, thinking of the terror in Eddie's eyes when he realized his mother was coming for him, I started to cry. God, I thought, why should these kids suffer so terribly? Nothing I could ever do for Eddie, no warmth or kindness I could ever show him, would negate his mother's cruelty.

I was still crying when I left the building. My car was the only one left on the lot. It was getting dark early now, and as the freezing wind cut through me I felt as if I were the last person on earth. I drove home slowly, not yet ready to resume my responsibilities there. When I finally pulled into the driveway, I sat still, watching the falling snow gleam in the headlights. I was purged of tears, but exhausted and discouraged.

# CHAPTER 14

Eddie came back three days later, ugly bruises on his arms and back. "My bottom's worse. It's all purple. She hit me with her belt. Here, keep these." He handed me a rumpled paper bag, full of his mother's belts. "I'm never bringing them back."

He ran in wide circles around the furniture. "I've been locked in my room since Tuesday. Didn't even get any supper. Oh . . . Oh . . . I hate being locked up! I hate her whipping me! I wanna knock the whole damn house down. I wanna crush it with a bulldozer! I wanna get matches and burn it!" He was still running.

"No wonder you can't sit, Eddie. Run around three more times. Then we'll tell you the party plans."

The children watched sympathetically. He had circled twice when Julie asked solicitously, "Do you still have your gloves?"

"Oops, I forgot to leave them!" He headed for the office.

In his absence, Douglas said, "I'll put my coat on his chair so he can sit better."

"That's kind of you, Doug."

"Duty before pleasure."

"That's a mature attitude."

"Well, I'm nine. These other punks are younger."

"Uh-uh," objected Kevin. "I'm almost nine."

"Listen," Doug continued, "I'm nine and a half, and Julie and Kevin are still eight." Interestingly, he made no mention of Jonathan.

Eddie trotted in and thanked Douglas for cushioning his chair.

"Does Eddie know about next week?" Julie asked.

"Tell him."

"Next Tuesday we're having a class party. Everybody's supposed to bring a present. Wednesday we're having a party with mothers. Fathers too, if they can come. We practiced songs to sing and—"

"Oh no! You're not inviting my mother! I'm not getting whipped in school too!"

"And my mother's not coming either," Kevin added. "She's too busy."

"Maybe things will be different next week. Let's rehearse the songs again."

Even with sound effects, Douglas beating on a tom-tom, our rendition of *Drummer Boy* was miserable. If possible, *Dreidel, Dreidel* sounded worse.

"We should tell everybody what a dreidel is," Douglas suggested. "It says here on the music. A dreidel is a piece of clay, mow—moe—molded. . . ." His reading was still far from fluent.

Eddie interrupted, reciting the message perfectly.

Douglas was mortified. "I should say it. I'm the oldest! That little punk better stop his bragging."

Eddie dashed over to Douglas and yanked his chair out from under him. Douglas crashed to the floor, still in sitting position, then rose and socked Eddie in the stomach. Eddie collapsed, howling.

Douglas extended his hands, palms up, in supplication. "Don't blame me, Mrs. Craig. You saw the little punk started it."

"Of course, I blame you. I blame both of you. You both know by now there are better ways to solve problems. What do you prove when you hurt each other? Does it settle anything?"

"Oh, taking the punk's side, huh?" Douglas shoved his desk into the familiar corner. Again Kevin followed piously.

"Here, boog." Eddie, suddenly recovered, flung Douglas' jacket at him. "Take this with you. I'm not sitting on your bugs."

The rest of the day went badly for Eddie. He cried that his bruises hurt, ran wildly, and frequently provoked Douglas into punching him.

As soon as he left, I called Ceil at the administration building.

"We've got to do something quickly. Eddie's mother is just working at cross purposes to us—locking him up, beating him, making him desperate to hurt someone else. Now he's encouraging attacks on himself, as if he wants pain."

"Look, I agree with you. But I have to run to a meeting. Would you call her and set up an appointment for all three of us to meet? Let me know when, and I'll be there. She's got to be told how detrimental it is to lock him up. Talk to you later."

But I made no appointment with Eddie's mother. When I asked her to come in as soon as possible, she replied, "Well, in the case of my son, he has a pattern to his life. A rhythm. I do too. It takes us a long. . . ." Her voice trailed off as if she were floating away.

"Mrs. Conte, Mrs. Black and I would like to talk to you about Eddie. He's been having a hard time in school. When could we see you?"

"I don't know why everyone tells me to lock him in his room." She continued. "He's begun talking to himself in there. And when they tell me to whip him, they're making me treat him like an animal."

"Mrs. Conte," I felt desperate. "Listen, please. Beating him and locking him up will make Eddie worse. We want to help you find other ways to handle him. What day could you come in?"

"I know exactly what happened and where and how," she continued, ignoring my question. "He has all this in him. He has to find himself. I know how hard it is because I was lost for years. I want to say—" a long pause—"thanks for calling." Click.

# CHAPTER 15

The following Tuesday was our class party. It began at noon, with everyone eating lunch together at the round table.

The boys wore everyday school clothes, but Julie dressed for the occasion, in pink organdy and lace-trimmed sleeves.

Eddie noticed. "You look pretty, Julie."

"It's my goodest dress. Mrs. Craig, do you like me all glamored up? Do my things show?"

"Ha-ha," Eddie roared. "What things? You don't have any titties!"

"Your dress is lovely, Julie," I said. "Why don't you be first at the grab bag?"

The gift Kevin had surreptitiously deposited in the carton under the tree was the only one with a name tag. Julie picked it, not realizing whom it was from. The label read G R I L.

"This one says girl. It must be for me. I'm the only girl." She tore through layers of green tissue until a tinny ring with a green stone, genus gum machine, lay exposed. Even when Kevin began to squirm, no one connected him with the gift.

Julie put it on her left hand, then gazed admiringly.

"Who are you marrying?" Eddie asked.

"Oh, silly, I'm not really getting married," she giggled. "Anyway I'm not ever getting married in my whole life. You won't catch me standing in front of a minister so long, saying all those words, in high heels that'll hurt my feet."

Eddie got a squirt gun in the grab bag, Jonathan crayons, and Douglas Play-Doh. Kevin refused to take his gift. Eddie opened it for him. "Here, Kevin, you get a comic. It's the *Fantastic Four.*"

"Uh-uh. It's not for me. If I bring it home, my mother can save it for my brother, or Douglas can have it."

"Hey, thanks pal," Douglas took the magazine.

The P.T.A. contributed ice cream cups and fancy cookies. Everyone ate eagerly except Kevin, who rejected his ice cream by shoving it in front of Douglas.

Douglas, having launched into a story, finished his own dessert and immediately ate his way through Kevin's, quite unaware of how it got there.

"You should be glad I'm here today," he was saying. "I coulda been locked up in jail."

Wooden ice cream spoons halted in mid-air. Julie gasped.

"It's like this." He warmed to his audience. "Me and another kid got caught in Woolworth's yesterday. The manager called the police."

"Wow! What'd ya do?" Eddie asked in admiration.

"Well, me and my friend, we was trying to look like salesmen so we could sneak out with this Jaguar model. It was gutsy, man, only it was too big to hide." He shot me a penetrating you-made-me-do-it look, then continued. "So the manager took us to his office, and the cop came to talk to us. We thought he was gonna arrest us."

"Piggy cop," Eddie sneered.

"Piggy cop nothin', man. We coulda gone to the station. You don't think anybody's gonna stand still for two little punks like me and my friend, do you?"

"Hey, where's my ice cream?" Kevin suddenly demanded.

"You pushed it over for Douglas, remember?" I replied.

"I didn't mean to give it to him. I take it back."

Douglas was lapping the last sip of melted vanilla from the container.

"Too late, I'm afraid. Douglas finished it. I'll get you another one."

"Oh, no. I want my own."

"Don't think you're ever coming over, Doug." Kevin was punishing. "I've got two places to go. Saturday and Sunday. All day."

"I'm going someplace too." Everyone stared at Jonathan, so unexpected was his participation in any conversation.

"I've got a new kind of doctor I'm going to. A kiatrist. He wears glasses. I know they're X-ray. He can see right through me."

"What's his name?" I asked.

"Dr. Russell."

"He's a good doctor." I made a mental note to ask Dr. Russell if Jonathan might examine those glasses.

"Kevin shouldn't get mad, should be, Mrs. Craig? How could Douglas know it was his ice cream?" Logic from Julie, the least acceptable source, was enough to drive Kevin right into the closet. He pulled the door shut as well.

"Oh, Kevin, now you're being a baby." Julie was relentless.

"Kevin wants to be alone a little while. We'll leave his ice cream here. He'll probably be ready for it soon."

"He'll never eat it," Julie said. "Kevin is just like me. We both like to get ourselves in trouble."

"You like to get in trouble?" I repeated.

"That's because I don't like myself." She continued. "Sometimes I try to hurt myself. I could even kill myself!"

Douglas reached for another cookie. "Julie is her own persecutor. Kevin too. Not me, man! Other people persecute me, but I'd never do it to myself."

"Well, you like yourself," Julie said. "That's different."

"Ya, well my grandmother likes me too," said Douglas. "Please don't tell her, but she likes me more than my brother. Anyway, my brother fell on a rock and died, so he won't he here tomorrow. Just my grandmother's coming."

Eddie hopped up. "Don't worry about my mother. She won't be coming either. She has to stay home all the time now and guard the house so my father won't sneak in." Eddie clutched his pants. "I have to go to the bathroom. Be right back."

"My brother's not really dead. Just his brain is dead." Douglas seemed to be speaking to himself.

"It's hard to have a retarded brother," I said, trying to bring him back.

Eddie returned quickly with a question for Doug. "Is it okay if I called the kid in the bathroom a nigger?"

The inquiry further depressed Douglas. His response was barely audible. "Don't do it, Ed. Don't pick on any black kid. They've had enough pickin' on already."

We played musical chairs. Eddie stormed back to his desk when he was first to lose, and Douglas knocked both chairs over when he was second out. That left two at the party, that is, two and Kevin's shoes, which he had slipped into the room. I acknowledged that it was good to see them and hoped Kevin would join us too. But Julie scolded, "It's stupid, Kevin. Your shoes in here without you."

A muted response from the closet. "Think I'm stupid, how about you?"

Kevin did come out when it was time to leave, but sniffed and turned away when I said good night.

After supper that night I tried to help Billy with his arithmetic, but couldn't keep my mind off tomorrow's party. Inviting the parents had been a foolish mistake. I was putting unfair pressure on the children, expecting too much too soon. They had enough trouble relating to one another and to me.

"Is twelve right, Mom?" Billy asked, and I was distressed to realize that I didn't even know what problem he was doing.

I couldn't sleep that night despite Bill's assurance that the party would undoubtedly go smoothly. "Besides," he reasoned, "if the kids don't behave, it won't come as any surprise to their parents."

On Wednesday morning I went in early to fix up the classroom, then realized with dismay that the cans of punch sat on our porch at home. Before I could decide what to do, Julie and Eddie burst in, breathless. "Douglas was on the bus, but he says he's not coming in!" Again I felt the frustration of having no one with whom to leave the group so I could look for him.

But shortly after Kevin and Jonathan straggled in, Douglas arrived, triumphantly holding aloft a startled tiger cat. "Look what I found! She must be lost. She was under a bush in front of the building. Isn't she fat?"

Eddie lifted the animal's front paws and examined her stomach. "She's having babies, dummy."

"Oh, and she's lost! Can we keep her, Mrs. Craig? Please? Please?" At last, a unanimous request.

"Shh, you'll frighten her. She looks too well-cared-for to be lost. She probably lives near the school. Our guests will be here at eleven, so perhaps we could keep her in the room until ten-thirty. If she's still around after school, we'll decide what to do with her."

"Can we make her a bed?" Doug begged. A storage carton was quickly emptied of workbooks. Each child insisted on contributing his coat as a mattress. The gentle cat was placed inside, and a fight broke out as each pulled at the box to keep it near his desk.

"She'll want to leave if you don't stop! We'll decide on turns by drawing anagrams as we've done before."

Douglas drew C and was first. Eddie, with M, had last turn and had to wait until ten-fifteen. At about ten-twenty, Julie and I were arranging cookies when Douglas remarked, "Will wonders never cease, the way Eddie is acting."

Eddie was holding the cat above his head, lapping her underside with his tongue. "I wanna suck your milk! Let me! Let me suck your milk!"

The cat meowed. I returned her to the box. "That's upsetting her, Eddie." He looked so agitated that I was afraid he was fantasizing. Suddenly he yelled, "Who's that giant at the door?"

There stood Bill with the cans I had forgotten.

"Oh, thank you so much for bringing the punch! Meet Douglas, Jonathan, Eddie, Julie, and Kevin. This is Mr. Craig."

Douglas waved a casual greeting. Jonathan belched five times. Kevin lowered his head. Julie leaped up and hugged Bill around the waist.

Eddie was coolest. "Mr. Craig, come see our cat." Bill smiled and walked to his desk. "Bend down, Mr. Craig. Take a good look."

Something in his tone warned me. "Bill don't." But I was too slow. Eddie wound up and socked him on the nose. Bill was stunned. His nose smarted, and tears sprang to his eyes. I could see his fists clenching as he fought the impulse to deal with Eddie directly.

Bill had regained his composure before I reached them. He put his arm around the small boy's shoulder. "Hey, you know that wasn't fair. I thought you really wanted me to see the cat."

"Listen!" Eddie was upset. "Don't you understand I can't control myself?" he screamed.

"That sounds like a cop-out, pal. Who's supposed to control you if not yourself? You're not hitting anybody right now, are you? You're proving you can control yourself. Think it over."

Bill agreed to take the cat out with him. Julie insisted on kissing him good-bye. He spoke briefly to each boy and privately to me at the door. "Interesting group you've got here." We both smiled, and he walked toward the exit with the bulging cat under his arm.

A few minutes later Mrs. Bergman, Jonathan's mother, stood hesitantly at the door. She had on the same stained coat she wore the first day Jonathan had come to school.

Douglas, pulling his rank as oldest, had appointed himself official greeter and led her to the chairs he had arranged earlier.

The unhappy-looking woman offered a strained smile as she passed Jonathan. "Hello, son." Flushed with embarrassment, he jumped up yelling, "Oh! Ow! A tack in my butt! Burp-urp. Calling AO-5. Someone broke the radar barrier! On guard!" His mother's eyes filled with tears.

Mrs. Conte came next, with Eddie's five-year-old sister clutching a leg of her mother's purple pants suit. The room became unnaturally quiet. Both children and parents looked ill at ease.

Julie's and Kevin's mothers arrived together, chatting amiably. At exactly eleven, Douglas' grandmother and his brother Luke stood at the door. Douglas did not offer escort across the room. I caught his stricken look and went to them. Nothing had prepared me for Luke's sad condition. He was spastic as well as retarded. He stepped with his left foot then dragged the right side of his body. Grandmother's guiding hand firmly clasped his frail wrist. His mouth hung open and his tongue protruded, but his eyes shone when he saw Douglas.

I introduced the women, who exchanged self-conscious greetings. Frequently and with great confidence, Eddie had practiced standing in front of the room to announce the songs. Now, head bowed, frozen in his chair, he muttered the words. That was the cue for the children.

They rose reluctantly and stood behind Julie, who with trembling hand spun the dreidel. Eddie and Douglas, eyes fixed on me, were the only ones whose voices were audible. Jonathan grimaced, rolled his eyes, and deliberately struck his hand against the blackboard behind him. Jumping on one foot he wrung his hand in mock agony.

When the song was done, Jonathan fled to his seat and holding invisible instruments began long involved surgery on the imaginary wound. His mother, chin quivering, focused her eyes straight ahead. The other woman stared as the operation progressed from initial incision through suturing.

Douglas, as planned, picked up the drum and began tapping an introduction to the next song. At first the singers were timid, too weak to be effective, but as their confidence increased so did the volume. Their voices were pure and lilting as they sang, "I am a poor boy too . . ." to Douglas' drum.

Ceil tiptoed in and stood at the back of the room. We exchanged glances, and she put her hand to her throat as if having difficulty swallowing. I knew she felt as I did.

There was a brief silence followed by applause. Kevin looked embarrassed, but the others were delighted. Douglas made a spontaneous speech: "Me and the kids and Mrs. Craig are glad you came. If you liked our songs, there's some food back there."

Douglas raced Julie and Eddie to the refreshments. With prompting, they served the guests first. Douglas sipped from both of the cups he carried to his grandmother and brother. Kevin looked longingly toward the closet, his favorite retreat, then headed in that direction.

"Here, Kevin," I said, trying to divert him, "this is for your mother and you." He took the cups and went to his mother. Eddie now sat clinging to his mother, as did his sister on her other side. Mrs. Conte smoked and looked bored. When Eddie tugged at her, she snapped, "Will you kids stop buggin' me?"

Jonathan was still closing his wound. With intense concentration he wielded the nonexistent needle.

Aware of Mrs. Bergman's distress, Ceil engaged her in conversation. Through the chatter in the room, I briefly heard Jonathan's mother saying, "I don't understand what he's doing today. At home he's such a good boy. I just had my difficult time of the month, you know, and I'm always so sick the whole week before. But Jonathan brings me cups of tea and does all the dusting. He's usually so sweet."

The party lasted forty-five minutes. To Julie's delight, her mother and Kevin's had a long conversation, forcing Kevin to be grouped with her. The pleasure-pain principle was never better illustrated than by his face.

I offered cookies to Eddie's sister, who shrank away. Eddie, too, suddenly acted afraid of me. His eyes showed no recognition as he clung to his mother.

Jonathan never did join the party. When his mother finally approached him, asking if he wanted a drink, he burped in response and continued to wrap his hand in what would have been miles of bandage.

Douglas remained with his brother and grandmother. She was a picture in a starched white cotton dress, her hair pinned in a bun, her dark skin glistening.

Luke's hand shook as he raised the cup to his mouth. Juice streamed down his plaid flannel shirt. As though he had done it a thousand times, Douglas took the cup and held it to his brother's lips.

Mrs. Bergman was the first to leave. She looked shaken as she wished Ceil and me happy holidays. Jonathan screamed when she pulled at his arm and tried to make him move more quickly. "Ow! Ow! You don't think it hurts!"

Julie and her mother helped clean up the room. Julie deposited paper cups in the wastebasket, while Mrs. Neumayer wiped the tabletops. Julie hugged and kissed me. Kevin did not answer when I wished him a happy vacation.

Saying good-bye to Eddie's mother afforded an opportunity to ask again for a conference. Hand on her hip she stared me down before answering. "Well, I'll letcha know if I can come."

Ceil moved in. "We have to be more definite, Mrs. Conte. We could meet the Friday after vacation. Let's see, that would be January eighth." Mrs. Conte glared at Ceil, snapped her chewing gum, sauntered out. The children, alarmed that she left without them, ran after her.

With the others gone, Douglas became his more ebullient self. "Hey, did I do good on the drums?"

"You were great!"

"Well, have a nice Christmas, Mrs. Craig. You too, Mrs. Black."

"It's happy Hanukkah to me, Doug." Ceil smiled.

"Oh, you Jewish? I coulda been too, you know.

Roses are red,
Violets are bluish.
If it wasn't for Christmas,
We'd all be Jewish."

Ceil and I laughed.

His grandmother was wiping Luke's hands and face with a paper napkin. "Douglas, you take him outside now."

"Good-bye, Luke," I said. "Bye, Douglas. I'll see you in ten days. Have a nice Christmas."

Luke limped out, looking happy to be holding his brother's hand.

"I want to thank you both," the grandmother smiled, "for puttin' my boys' names on that list for presents. They don't expect nothin'."

"It should be a happy Christmas," I said.

"They gonna have miseries too." The old woman shook her head sadly. "That man my daughter ran away with, he back to his wife. I'm afraid their mother be comin' back too. She'll hurt those boys all over if she come back and then leave 'em again."

Ceil said, "Mrs. Grant, even though it's vacation, I'll be in my office next week. You can reach me there if there's any way I can help. If your daughter should return, I'd be glad to talk to her."

"No," she replied softly, "nothin' nobody can do."

When she left, I confronted Ceil with a question that had been bothering me. "Why hasn't anyone done something for Luke? Don't the schools have a program for him? Shouldn't he be with the educable or trainable retarded?"

"Maybe, but we have to take one step at a time. Even though Douglas was out of school most of last year, it took a lot of preparation to get Mrs. Grant's consent to his being in this class. She gets upset by any mention of Luke. I think she's afraid we'll send him away. We want to be sure we have her confidence before discussing Luke again. Otherwise we might jeopardize Douglas' being here."

We talked about Jonathan's "operation," Eddie's behavior with his mother, and the possible effects on Luke and Douglas if their mother did return.

"Perhaps," I wished aloud, "she's had her fling. She must have been terribly desperate with those little ones, especially Luke, and no husband to share the burden. If she does come home, and we could help with Luke, it might change the picture for all of them."

"On that hopeful note, and with the realization that you and I could talk forever, let your vacation officially begin." She raised a cup of punch.

"Happy Hanukkah, Ceil."

"Merry Christmas, El."

Christmas vacation meant lots of ice skating and leisurely family breakfasts. Bill took time off too, for the book was nearing completion earlier than he had expected.

Bill tried to tell the kids that there would be fewer presents this year, but Ann interrupted before he finished. "We already knew that, Dad. Don't worry, we'd rather have your book."

I was proud and relieved, but the children's reaction depressed Bill. "I've been terribly selfish," he said, "making everyone sacrifice so I can do what I want."

"Honey, it's what we *all* want." I really meant it.

"I'll tell you one thing," he said, "if this book doesn't do well, I'll go right back to selling. I'll never try writing again."

## CHAPTER 16

We went back to school on January fifth. During the vacation I was absorbed in Bettelheim, Gesell, and Axline, and returned to school with a sense of renewal, proud to be teaching the Transitional Class.

The minute the outside door opened, I could hear them fighting. Thus ended all hope of a fresh start.

"You black!" Eddie was yelling. "You and your whole family are black bastards!"

"It's about time you picked on me, you little girl picker," Douglas replied.

"Just because Julie cries, you think she's perfect," Kevin complained.

The group made little progress down the hall, but their voices echoed everywhere.

"At least Julie gets gooder grades than you two," said Douglas.

Eddie defended himself. "I'm in a higher book!"

Such evidence was wasted on Douglas. "Huh, she tries at least."

"Kevin," Julie was still crying, "you cause the trouble. You tell Eddie to hurt me."

"So what, crybaby?"

"You did tell me to punch her, Kevin," Eddie admitted.

"Stay offa my side, Eddie," Julie sniffed.

I met them at the door, allowing each one into the room except Kevin, who was dragging behind.

I blocked his entry with my arms and let him have it, in a subdued voice to keep the others from hearing.

"I'm sick of you getting other people to do your dirty work,

Kevin. We both know you start these things, and you're going to stop."

He covered one ear and whispered, "I'm not listening."

"You better listen. If you're angry, from now on, say it. Stop using other people."

He ducked under my arm, put his things away, and sat very quietly.

I said to the group. "Let's not begin the new year with an argument. Let's think, instead, what we can do to prevent these problems."

A long pause. No suggestions.

"Die," Eddie murmured.

"Then we'll talk about it again." I went on. "For now, just consider your own part—what you should do, what you should stop doing, to make our room a happier place. We haven't been together for a while. What did you do last week?"

"Miss you," Douglas answered.

"Got a bike!" Jonathan enthused.

"My cousin got a bike," said Kevin.

"Oh, you should see what my mother got from my father! He's her boyfriend, you know." Julie stood up to pose, hands low on her hips. "It's this beautiful negligee, cut up to here (pointing to her navel) with slits all around."

Eddie whistled appreciatively. Douglas and even Jonathan laughed. Kevin blushed.

"Hey guys!" Douglas cupped his hand to his mouth, "What do you do when a girl does this?" A hand signal.

"Oh boy!" pint-sized Eddie replied. "Take her into a dark alley, and then the fun begins."

"What fun?" Douglas was testing.

Eddie passed the exam. "Then you blip her."

"Hey yah, man!" The eight-year-old agreed.

Julie, no woman's-libber, looked flattered.

"You shoulda seen our place, Mrs. Craig," Douglas said. "Luke and me got a thousand presents."

"Well I didn't!" Eddie yelled. "My mother ruined our Christmas! My father brought us stuff, but she kicked him out. He was so mad, he took my train set! My sister's doll too!"

In a blur, Eddie was across the room, climbing the five shelves to the top of the bookcase. There he sat, knees huddled to his chin, looking more unhappy than defiant.

"I'll help you down, Eddie." I approached him cautiously, hoping he'd wait. But he jumped. The bookcase swayed and crashed to the floor, spewing books, games, and finger paints.

Even he was appalled at the mess. "I didn't mean it! I didn't mean it!"

"You didn't do it on purpose, Eddie, but that was a dangerous place to be. We'll ask Mr. Jakowsky to help clean up."

"Oh, no! He's not seeing this!" Eddie righted the shelves, rearranged the books, and scrubbed the floor while the class engaged in a full hour of quiet activities.

Jonathan broke the extraordinary silence. "I can't work with these kids making so much noise!" He pushed his paper off his desk. It floated onto Douglas' foot. Picking it up, Douglas gave it a solemn appraisal.

"Now I know what's wrong with that kid," he said. "Look at this shaky writing. He musta had a nervous breakdown."

He handed it to Jonathan sympathetically. "Don't worry. You'll be better soon, kid."

"Pow! Wow! Bam, bam, bam!" Jonathan replied.

By lunchtime everyone had read and had completed all their folders except Kevin, who still had one number paper left to do.

The others were smug, pitiless, as they strutted by him to get their lunches.

"Do you understand the work?" I sat beside him.

"Maybe I do. Maybe I don't."

"It's on pages eight and nine," I prompted.

"Hmm," he thumbed through the book, finally opening it on page eighty-nine. "There's your eight and nine!"

"You know better." I turned the pages. "Here's the first example. What's five and three?"

"Seven? Nine?"

He finally finished. "Get your lunch now. Doesn't it feel good to be done?"

"I could have finished faster alone."

While Kevin ate, the others selected toys for the afternoon.

"Uh-uh." Kevin whined, when Douglas picked the truck. "I holdsie that."

"You shouldn't play this afternoon, Kevin," Julie said. "You've been acting too bad."

"It's true, Mrs. Craig," Douglas agreed, hand on the truck. "He'll never hurry his work if you let him play anyway."

"But he finished. Don't you think he should play?" I asked.

"No! No!" they chorused.

"Stick to it, Mrs. Craig!" Douglas clutched the toy. "Unless you want to be a softy all your life."

"When Kevin has eaten, he's free to play," I said. "But he can't reserve the truck."

Douglas grinned in relief. "Boy, you can promote me, but there'll never be another teacher like you!"

Kevin still coveted the truck. "Remember, Doug, you want to come to my house?"

"Yeah," he looked up.

"Not if you act like a punk," Kevin threatened. "I can still tell my mother you threw my jacket out. She'd sue you."

"I'm not coming over," Douglas decided.

"So what?"

"Okay, I won't. It would be a pleasure."

The rest of that play period went smoothly. Certainly there was nothing to alert me to the disastrous days that lay ahead.

# CHAPTER 17

It was Friday. By nine forty-five no children had arrived. I went out, hoping to catch some sign of the bus. Suddenly, tires screeching, it careened into the parking lot. But no children were on it.

Mr. Dixon raged at me. "I warned 'em! I don't have to drive them bastards. They're gonna cause an accident! They kept fighting, so I threw 'em off."

He gunned the motor and whipped the bus around in a tight circle.

"Wait!" I jogged along, calling up to him. "Where did you leave them?"

"By Francis Street! Down about a mile!" He left and I ran in that direction, then realized the futility of it. From Francis Street, near Eddie's stop, there were several possible routes, if indeed the kids would head for school and providing they knew the way.

I hopped into my car, turned on the ignition, and again had second thoughts.

Miss Silverstein should know what happened, and possibly the police as well. Doris, the secretary, had no idea where Miss Silverstein went. By the time I located her on the second floor, I was so out of breath I could barely speak. After my brief tale, we rushed to her office.

Knowing I should be in class, Doris looked disappointed when the principal closed the door to her private office.

"Both the police and the bus company must be alerted," she said. "I wonder if that driver realizes he's responsible for whatever happens."

Miss Silverstein had begun dialing when we heard the stamping in the hall, followed by Douglas' wail, "Mrs. Cra-a-a-aig!"

He spotted me and collapsed like the movie version of a victim of the desert.

"The others," he moaned feebly, "are coming."

The words were barely spoken when Eddie appeared. "Mr. Dixon kicked us off the bus. That bitch! I hate him!"

"And the others?" I asked.

"Kevin is comin'. Jonathan and Julie are way back."

Eddie dropped next to Douglas. They lay panting in the middle of the hall. Miss Silverstein arrived on the scene while I was urging the boys to move. "You could get stepped on here."

In came Kevin, every freckle intensified by his deathly pallor and starched white shirt. "Jonathan—fell—down. Cut—his—knee. Julie's with him."

"I'll go after them," Miss Silverstein said.

Kevin and I led the procession to our room. Douglas and Eddie followed, on hands and knees all the way.

"Put your heads down and rest a while," I said.

After a few peaceful moments, Eddie looked up. "Are you gonna fire the bus driver?"

The boys' breathing became more labored as they remembered their suffering.

"I can't promise till I know exactly what happened," I said.

Each, suddenly revitalized, launched into his version of the morning's ride.

In the midst of the babble, Miss Silverstein stood at the door. "Jonathan's in the nurse's office getting a Band-Aid on his knee. Julie," she hugged the girl, "was like a nurse herself. She was taking such good care of Jonathan when I found them."

The principal left.

"Thank you, Julie," I said.

"You're thanking bug-eyes?"

Kevin's remark was drowned in yet another swell of protest against Mr. Dixon. Douglas stood and faced his classmates. Raising his hands above his head, he commanded silence.

"Listen, I'm the oldest!"

The oldest was not the cleanest. He was a comical figure, his striped jersey, blue jeans, nose, cheeks, and hands smudged with dirt from crawling on the floor.

"I say Mrs. Craig tells the superintendent of schools we're *never* ridin' Bus 10 again."

"Yah!"

"Tell him!"

"He threw us off. Said he'd like to kick our—"

"Just a minute," I said. "I'll need something in writing if you expect me to submit a protest."

With a frown of concern, Douglas dispensed both paper and advice. "Be gutsy. We've gotta convince him."

They were writing when the nurse brought Jonathan in. His face, shirt, and tan jacket were tear-stained, but my sympathy was tempered by the thought that it was good for him to have received Julie's attention.

"You've had a hard morning," I said. "How's your leg?"

He began crying again. "More trouble. Prehistoric monsters living in our drain! There since the Mesozoic Age."

"Now, Jonathan, that's impossible. Your drain isn't that old. Will you ask your dad to check it?"

"I told him, but he doesn't believe me!"

I was still comforting Jonathan when the first two anti-bus driver depositions were completed and handed to me by the somber authors.

After lunch, Julie expressed the apprehension they all felt. "How will we get home, Mrs. Craig? Mr. Dixon might kick us out again."

"Let me speak to Miss Silverstein, and then I'll answer." I picked up the intercom, planning to ask permission to drive the children home. The principal had other news.

"The bus company called. Mr. Dixon walked in a while ago and threw his keys on the boss' desk. The manager says he'll drive till there's a replacement."

The children were visibly relieved when I told them. "We knew you wouldn't make us ride with that bum," said Douglas.

I was pleased with this expression of confidence and even more with the realization that, given a choice, they all had headed directly for school!

1 I think the busDrive should be Replaced
2 He is meen To us,
3 He Dont like us
4 we Dont like Him
5 He threw us off the bus
6 He swore

→ → → →

by

Eddie

I hate
him!
I hate him!
I hate hil Bun

I hatem I
We hate himhate him

Douglas

1. We think the bus driver Should be replaced.

2. Becous he Swairs.

3. Becous heis to ruDe!.

4. And Becaus he tris to Butter US UpsAnd heis Cranke!
6. he Shots At Us
7. And he Said get out You dirty fucking thing
8. When I got of the Bus →

heKick's US Up And US Out And I got A cut By him

We hat him

But that illusion of progress was short-lived. For the rest of the month and well into February, each child's condition worsened.

Jonathan constantly talked to his pencils or scolded crayons for jumping around in his desk. Still fascinated with holes, he spent days trying to drill through his desktop and then through the blackboard. In one week he was sent home twice for soiling.

Julie ran the gamut of her psychosomatic complaints. "Does my neck look swollen?" or "I think I'm getting a rash." She bit herself up and down her arms until she was covered with bruises. She chewed her hair and clung to me at every opportunity.

As for Douglas, his tantrums in January were nearly as terrible as the outbursts to which he had first subjected Kevin and me. Without warning, he would rip and shred the wall charts and room decorations, all so time-consuming to re-do. In enormous letters he wrote "FUCK" on the blackboard every time he got near it.

Sometimes, after the havoc, he would offer a belligerent excuse. "Look, what d'ya expect? See? This is the way I slept all night, with my head hanging over the side of the bed."

Yet I knew that Douglas, who seemed so much more difficult on the surface, was better off than Kevin. Douglas punched and kicked, yelled and cried. He had outlets for his anger, and I hoped that he would eventually express it more appropriately.

But Kevin, beneath his passive exterior, harbored as much if not more hostility, and worse, could rarely channel it even in a primitive way. These pent-up feelings interfered with his learning. Not daring to be aggressive, he was far less ready for reading and arithmetic than Douglas.

Only in his negativism was Kevin becoming more overt. I found myself repeating, "If you won't look, I can't explain this to you." Now he was responding, "Isn't that too bad."

Julie was Kevin's most distressing problem in school. As much as her hugging me bothered him, he was even more uncomfortable when she dallied in the closet to comb her hair. The sketches on his folders revealed the agitation she caused him.

But of all the children, I was more concerned about Eddie. He had begun having what I could only describe to Ceil as seizures. With no apparent provocation he would suddenly slump

*Sketch on Kevin's Folder*

to the floor and lie face down, his eyes closed. I tried speaking to him, both comfortingly and later imperatively. His only response was to blink rapidly. If I pulled him up, as soon as my support was withdrawn he slumped back to the floor.

At first this behavior lasted a minute or two, but soon it increased to twenty minutes and occurred several times a day. After each episode he acted dazed and apparently had no memory of what had happened.

Once Miss Silverstein happened to be present. Even her authoritative words "Get off the floor immediately!" triggered no reaction from Eddie.

Ceil too was alarmed. "We're due for a conference with Dr. Bialek soon. Let me try to set it up immediately so we can get his opinion."

We met the following Wednesday at the local Child Guidance Center, of which Dr. Norman Bialek was director. Ceil and I sat across from his huge desk while the psychiatrist unabashedly relished the remains of his lunch, a succulent golden pear.

The doctor was the epitome of his profession—charming, handsome, with a thick Viennese accent. While he enjoyed the pear, we told him about Eddie. Then he tilted back in his chair.

"I will have to see this boy. Perhaps we will want to do more testing on him. First, may I visit your class?"

"Please do."

"I'll be there Monday, February sixth, at about ten."

# CHAPTER 18

On the morning Dr. Bialek was to come, I made sure the children's assignments required little explanation. I wanted to be available if he had any comments.

When I put the folder on Eddie's desk, he tossed it back. "It's your work! You do it!"

"It's not my work, Ed."

"Well, you're the marker. Give me any mark you want."

"I don't get this junk!" Kevin said.

"Be with you as soon as I'm finished here, Kevin."

Julie began to pout. "You help Kevin more than you help me. You never let me ask you things. You only let the boys."

"Now, Julie, you know better. It will be your turn right after Kevin's."

But Kevin's feet were drowning me out in a heel-toe protest against having to wait.

"You little punk!" Eddie sprang at Kevin. "You're not getting away with that. I can't think when your feet are yelling." Eddie had both hands around Kevin's neck.

"We do not hurt people" I pulled Eddie away.

"Oh yeah?" Eddie spun to face me. "Nobody—nobody—can stop me from losing my temper."

"Just one person, Eddie. Nobody but you."

I hadn't noticed Dr. Bialek enter, but he was standing at the back of the room and had only a brief wait to observe Eddie's bizarre behavior.

I was holding Eddie's wrist to prevent him from punching Kevin, when he slumped to the floor and lay there writhing. His tongue was protruding, and he made guttural sounds—"Ahhh, ugggh."

The other children had seen this before. Only Jonathan still found it disconcerting. He whistled, talked to himself, made shooting noises, and burped.

"Jonathan," I bent to him, "Eddie will be all right."

"Pow! Pow!"

Dr. Bialek came closer for a better view of the prostrate boy.

Suddenly the convulsive motions stopped. His head flopped from side to side. His eyes rolled back so only the white showed. Then he was frighteningly still. I motioned to Dr. Bialek that I would pick him up, and he nodded in agreement.

Eddie was deadweight. I eased him into a chair. Once more I felt panicked by the uncertainty of whether he might be suffering a seizure. As though spineless, he slithered from his chair onto the floor. He lay face down, his eyes blinking incredibly rapidly. I tried all the techniques I had used before, so the psychiatrist could realize how futile they were.

While Eddie was still prone, Douglas demanded attention.

"Hey! Are you going to tell me now or not? Is this paper right?"

"It's fine, Doug." I looked over his shoulder. "Except that our is o-u-r not a-r."

"Why don't you go to hell?" he said.

"Just change that word. You'll be proud to have a perfect paper."

"It's my turn." Julie tugged at my sweater. "I've been waiting for you to help me."

Julie's question typified what a child with a perceptual problem might ask. "You don't mind if I do all my words in big letters, do you? I like big letters. They make me feel good."

"Big letters are easier, aren't they?" I said. "Some children get confused by little letters, especially b, d and p. I'll print the words for you, and you can copy them. Okay?"

Pleased with this, she finished quickly and was ready to do numbers. "Is this a nine or a six?"

Douglas, hand cupped over his mouth, spoke sotto voice. "Hey Kevin, did she say sex? Don't tell anyone, but did she?"

I had to smile. "Julie asked about the number six."

It spoiled his fun. "Don't be a square, Mrs. Craig. I'm not fixin' my paper either." He tore it up.

"Would you hand me the scraps, please?" I said. "Today's papers go on the bulletin board."

Fuming, he kicked his desk away. "You make me so mad!" Then he stalked to the front of the room, snatched a fresh paper, and rewrote the work faultlessly.

Dr. Bialek coughed. I had forgotten all about him. We spoke quietly, near the door.

"After observing the boy," he nodded toward Eddie, still on the floor, "I'm convinced this is not a physical problem. I'm going to prescribe medication that should help calm him down. Something emotional, some internal stimulus is triggering this behavior. It is not in response to what is happening at the time when he does this. I'd like to talk to you and Mrs. Black again about him after we've tried the medication for a while. Let me know if it should make him drowsy. Call the clinic for an appointment in about three weeks. We'll have a chance to discuss the other children too."

Eddie recovered shortly after Dr. Bialek left, and soon challenged Douglas to see who would finish his assignments first. They were both done by eleven-thirty and played a quiet, thoroughly rigged game of Candy Land. Douglas blatantly stacked the cards to his advanatge, but if Eddie noticed he chose not to complain.

Kevin, irked by Douglas' attention to Eddie, painstakingly wrote down the opposite of his spelling words, "loose" for tight, "short" for tall, and so on.

"I feel like getting in trouble," he said for Douglas' benefit, "so I can stay home."

He barely finished correcting that paper by noon. Douglas and he ate lunch together regularly, and Kevin now placed his chair by his friend's. For the first time, Eddie asked, "Can I eat with you too?"

"If he does, I'll run out of the room," said Kevin.

Douglas was torn. "Maybe we should try to be friends."

"Uh-uh." Kevin was firm. "He never shows he likes me."

"If you keep blabbin' your mouth, he never will like you, and you won't have any friends."

Kevin shrugged. "I don't need any friends, Doug."

"Everybody does, Kev. Listen, Eddie, maybe you can eat with us some other time."

"You're all goddam bastards!" Eddie yelled. "I'm getting outta here."

For a while we ate in troubled silence, broken by Jonathan's comments to his lunch. "Whoops! Oh, hey banana, get back here!" He tossed the banana from hand to hand, reacting as if the fruit jumped by itself. Eddie ran back in and sat down to eat.

I harbored my own anxiety. I kept wondering what Dr. Bialek would have to say about the children and what he really thought of the way I had handled them.

We were still eating when the school's fire alarm began its relentless wail. Eddie, petrified, darted into the closet. Julie ran to me and buried her head in my blouse.

Douglas was annoyed. "Kevin and I are eating. We're not playing fire-drill games. You're with us, right Jonathan?"

"It's a state law." I had to yell. "You have no choice. Line up immediately."

Kevin relented and was first at the door.

"Okay, Benedict Arnold." Douglas glared at him. "When I get you I'm gonna bash you."

With my right hand I scooped Jonathan from his seat. With my left I yanked Eddie from the closet. Julie, whose arms were locked around my waist, was dragged along. I didn't feel victorious about Douglas joining us. He was obviously after Kevin.

By the time we reached the playground, the entire school had congregated at the far end, in assigned fire-drill positions. The children stood absolutely silent, in perfect rows. I felt all eyes on us as the disorderly Transitional Class crossed the blacktop.

Suddenly, Douglas picked up a branch lying on the melting snow and began to whip Kevin, who seemed so innocent and helpless in his bow tie and neat clothes. Kevin howled.

Shaking Julie off, I grabbed for Douglas, caught his hand and squeezed it. "I'll let go when you drop the stick and behave yourself." The heavy boy looked wild, shirttails flying, pants unzipped.

Teachers, administrators, and four hundred thirty children stared in horror.

"Help! She's killing me!" Douglas screamed, contorting in false agony. "I'm gonna sue! Listen America! Listen America! My teacher's a fink!" He dropped the stick. "I hate you," he said. "I wish you would die. Let go. I won't hit the traitor again."

Sirens! Engines hadn't come to previous fire drills. It sounded as if they stopped on the other side of the building, although from the playground we couldn't see.

"Do you think they're testing how quickly the trucks arrive?" I asked Mary Quill, who was monitoring her third graders.

"Don't kid yourself." She said in a low voice. "Mr. Jakowsky told me there was a fire in the boys' bathroom!"

I thought instantly of Eddie's brief disappearance from our room. He had looked so terrified when the alarm rang.

The damage must have been minimal. We filed into the building about five minutes later, few realizing that the drill had been more than routine.

The crisp air proved exhilarating for all except Douglas, who was deflated and depressed. He curled up under the round reading table, pulled his shirt over his head, and sobbed. If I spoke to him or moved in his direction, the sobs became screams.

He seemed to need the release of crying. I sat with the other children, and with sticks, string, and scraps we created mobiles. Even Kevin and Jonathan participated.

Eddie enjoyed the project, but I watched him anxiously, wondering if he would say anything, do anything, that would indicate he knew about the fire.

Suddenly I felt Douglas' presence behind me.

"You've really been sad," I said.

"I feel better now."

"We'd like you have you join us."

"Could I make one?" he asked. "I feel much calmer."

He was cutting out a piece of a peace symbol when Kevin began to agitate. "How come you don't hit me again, Douglas? Don't want to get in trouble with the teacher?"

"You've got a big mouth, kid." Douglas strung up his mobile.

Julie beckoned for me to bend down. She cupped her hands around my ear. "Did you hear that? It's the first time Douglas got teased and didn't have a tantrum."

"Good for you for noticing! Would you say it out loud so everyone can hear?"

Julie stood up primly. With both hands she held out the skirt of her plaid jumper, as if she were about to curtsy.

"I just told Mrs. Craig that Douglas didn't even lose his temper when Kevin teased him." She spoke in a babyish voice. "And that's the first time." Julie held her head high.

Douglas cleared his throat. He sat taller. "Thanks for the compliment."

Kevin went to the closet. He put on his fur-collared coat.

"Where are you going?" I asked.

"Home." He faced the wall.

"The bus will be here in a few minutes. First, it's your turn to erase the board tonight."

Surprisingly, he came out and picked up the eraser, but ran it in zigzag patterns over the chalk marks.

"That makes it worse," I said. "Erase it correctly, please."

Kevin never showed more anger. His body shook with rage. His arm trembled as he pointed to the list of jobs. "Th—that ch—chart says I—I d—do boards, and I d—did boards!"

"If it makes you so angry to do it twice, Kevin, you'll have to do a better job the first time."

With frenetic speed he did the job again, then hurled the eraser toward the open window. It missed, landing on top of the radiator instead.

I blocked his exit. "It's all right to be angry, Kevin. Everyone feels that way at times, but you're hurting yourself by the way you show it. It will be better for you when you can put it in words. Thank you for erasing the board. See you tomorrow."

No answer until he was out of sight. Then his voice provided the sound effects for an imaginary rifle. "Bang! Kew-kew! Pow! Got her!"

The rest of the boys had left while Kevin was erasing the board. Julie lingered behind. Having been praised for her earlier observation, she made yet another on parting.

"Did you notice? Douglas is getting better. Kevin is getting worse."

"Don't worry about Eddie having set the fire," Ceil said shortly after Julie left. "Mr. Jakowsky caught a fifth grader in there smoking. The boy went back later and threw a match in the wastebasket. He's admitted it."

"What a relief!" I said. "Eddie doesn't need any more problems! Dr. Bialek saw him in action this morning. Said those episodes are emotional rather than physical, but he's putting him on a drug to calm him down. How do you feel about Eddie being medicated?"

Ceil paused. "We don't really know what long-term effects this kind of medication will have on children, either physiologically or to the personality. It's so dangerous to establish the precedent for the child that when things don't go well he can pop a pill in his mouth. Yet I think it's worth trying in this case. This boy needs to be less tense. It may also help him be more available for learning. We'll certainly want him off of it as soon as possible."

She frowned and continued. "A while ago I saw a five-year-old who'd been on medication since he was two and a half, for temper tantrums! That kind of abuse makes me angry—and frightened!"

# CHAPTER 19

In March the school's boiler broke down. Outside it was twenty degrees above zero, and the temperature inside was rapidly dropping. The children and I, teeth chattering, bundled in scarves and coats while the custodian determined the extent of the problem.

We played strenuous games to keep warm until finally the pipes in the old building began clanging as the steam forced its way through. Our room alone remained cold.

I sent for Mr. Jakowsky, who limped in with an assortment of tools projecting from his overalls. He stretched out on his back under the recalcitrant radiator and began tapping gently on the pipes.

The children, unaffected by his presence, continued their game of "Simon Says" until, without warning, the room erupted. Kevin had called Eddie "out."

"Liar! Liar!" Eddie was enraged. "Everyone here hates me!"

"Right!" said Douglas.

Eddie socked Kevin in the stomach. Kevin collapsed. Douglas ran after Eddie.

Suddenly a voice boomed from under the radiator. Startled, Eddie and Douglas halted in mid-chase as if frozen in motion.

"You kids, you!" Mr. Jakowsky pulled his head out from beneath the pipes. He sat up. "Look at me!" His face was scarlet. "I never had no nice teacher to help me. You wanna be like me? You wanna fix pipes when you grow up?"

The class was hushed.

Mr. Jakowsky shook his wrench at them. "You wanna mop floors all your lives? Spend every day cleaning other people's messes? You better sit down and listen to your teacher."

They tiptoed to their desks. Mr. Jakowsky returned to his work.

Minutes passed before Eddie, in a choked voice, broke the silence. "Don't blame me. I'm sick, ya know. And I didn't get my pill today, so I'm nervous."

"Eddie," I knelt to tell him privately, "you can control yourself without a pill."

The radiator began to hiss. The custodian pocketed his tools and left.

Other upsets that day were shorter and less intense than usual. Several times I noticed the boys, particularly Douglas and Eddie, gazing thoughtfully at the pipes.

Many of the children at Central School made no secret of calling my room the "nut factory" and eyed me and my pupils warily. But over the months a few seemed gradually to recognize it as a haven and began dropping in before and after school, ostensibly to talk and look around. The most regular of these were Paul and Sharon. They were waiting when I arrived the following morning.

Paul's before school visits had begun in February. The only child of a physician, he was one of the few from a small area in the school district with tree-lined streets and private houses.

At first he stopped by every few days to ask if he could wash the board or empty the wastebasket. Then I noticed Sharon, a waif-like six-year-old black girl, lingering in the hall. One day she followed Paul in. Now they both appeared daily and stayed until the second bell. Since our class operated on a different schedule, they never were there with my pupils.

This morning, Paul kept washing the board while I hung up my coat. Neither he nor Sharon responded to my greeting. If anything, they worked more avidly, as if reproaching me for being later than usual. Sharon rearranged books. Paul sponged the chalk tray. I was at my desk when he finally spoke.

"Some kids say your room is for crazies."

I looked up at the intense, intelligent face. Behind horn-rimmed glasses, his eyes narrowed, as if he were judging me.

"Do you think it's for crazies?"

He shook his head. "They couldn't be. Crazies wouldn't be able to work. But how come you don't have more kids?"

"Maybe next year I will. This is a new kind of program. The class is small so the children can get more help."

Sponge in hand, he approached my desk. "Maybe, could I come in sometime? The kids in my room are so snobby. My teacher'd let me if you'd send a note. I could bring my rock collection or my microscope."

"That's a nice offer, Paul. I'll check with your teacher about a date." The bell rang. "See you later."

He left, but Sharon kept working at the bookcase. She seemed to have something on her mind. Until recently she had barely spoken. Now each day she waited until we were alone. Her stories would tumble out in those stolen moments between Paul's departure and the late bell.

"Bemember I tole you my father tried to choke me?" she began, not looking up from her dusting. "Well, still I keep thinkin' 'bout him. He keep buyin' junk for his self, but he don't buy nothin' for our mother. He all mixed up, my father. I keep askin' my mother why did she marry him? She always say he ain't no good, and he ain't neither."

Sharon squatted and half-heartedly rearranged the games on the bottom shelf. "I keep thinking 'bout those people in China, too," she said. "They just get one drop of water and one drop of bread evvy day. But they lucky. They go in garbage cans, I bet. Our mother won't let us."

I could think of nothing to say to ease the burden this six-year-old carried. "It's very hard for children when their parents don't get along well, I know. But try to have a good day in school if you can."

She sighed, picked up her navy-blue sweater, and left for another session in first grade. I wondered how she could pay attention to anything any teacher said. I thought about her all day.

Driving home that afternoon I gradually began to realize that Sharon's and Paul's visits represented a kind of referral the Transitional Class Screening Committee had never anticipated. Weren't they silently seeking to be included with "the crazies?"

Because of the impending conference with Dr. Bialek, I tried to observe the children more closely than ever, especially Eddie. The psychiatrist would want to know his reaction to the medication.

For the first few days he was sluggish and listless, but by the second week his behavior was as erratic as before. He was far from drowsy the day of my conference with Dr. Bialek.

Before he entered he peeked in the room as if afraid of what he might find. Then he walked cautiously toward his desk, which he kept close to mine. I was amazed at the change in his appearance. Usually neat, he wore the same striped shirt and chino pants he had on the day before. The rumpled clothes looked slept in. His face and hands were filthy, his hair unkempt.

He pulled back his chair as if to sit down, but knocked it over. "Goddamnit! You know I don't like anyone touchin' my things! Who did this? That damn janitor?" He jumped up and down in the same spot, wailing. "I left my desk right against yours—now it's not even touching! Oh! Oh! I can't stand people moving my things! I'm going down to see Mrs. Black."

"It's not her day," I said. "She'll be here on Friday."

"Damn it!" He pounded both fists on the desk. "When I see her on Friday I'm going to kill her with a knife for not being here now."

As if Eddie did not exist, the children continued their routine of hanging up coats, putting away boots and lunchboxes. Only Julie, first in her chair, turned in his direction. She watched without expression.

"You're laughing at me! I see you. You're laughing at me!" He grabbed a ruler and fanned it in her face.

I appropriated the ruler. "You're upset this morning. What's wrong?"

"Oh, no! I'll never tell. I'm not supposed to tell, and you can't make me." He snatched a yardstick from the chalk tray and in a leap was on top of his desk brandishing the giant ruler like a sword.

"It looks as though you're not ready to be with us today." I approached him slowly.

"Oh no, no, Mrs. Craig!" He jumped down before I reached him. "Please don't send me home. I *can't* go home!"

"Then into the office till you show me you're calm enough to join the class."

Relieved, he took his work folder and pencils with him. The "office" no longer meant Miss Silverstein's. By rearranging furniture, I had isolated an extra desk between two bookcases. It faced a blank wall and was an effective "cooling off" place. I was pleased with this arrangement. Instead of being sent out of the room for hours, the child was separated only as long as necessary. Although Miss Silverstein was always understanding, I liked handling the discipline myself, without relying on her authority.

Eddie was barely settled when Kevin began the next disruption. There was a grapefruit-shaped bulge down the front of his green windbreaker. His hands cradled a mysterious object.

"Kevin brought a show-and-tell," Julie said.

Slowly, silently, without unzipping his jacket, he reached in and withdrew a crumpled paper bag. All eyes were on Kevin's hands as he opened the bag and pulled out a round plastic paperweight filled with imitation snow which drifted onto a miniature village.

Eddie, still in the "office," tilted his chair back so far to see that he was almost horizontal with the floor. "Gosh," he said, "that's beautiful!"

"Cool," Douglas agreed.

Julie reached toward Kevin. "Can I try it please?"

"Me first, old buddy," said Douglas.

A smile played on Kevin's lips. "Not Julie or Eddie or Jonathan. Just Douglas."

Julie began to whine.

Eddie kicked the wall. "Goddamnit! I want a turn!"

Jonathan continued drawing ghosts.

Douglas grabbed the paperweight, exclaimed as he created several snowstorms, and respectfully returned the treasure to Kevin, who slipped it back in the bag.

"How would you like it, Kevin," Julie reasoned, "if I didn't let you look in my viewer when I brought it?"

"Only Douglas," Kevin said, turning his shoulder, "you'd get cooties all over it."

Julie fled to the closet and wept into her coat.

"This is what we've talked about, Kevin," I said. "You're making trouble."

"He hates me!" Julie sobbed. "I know he hates me. Why doesn't he say so instead of hurting me?"

Kevin smiled.

Eddie yelled. "He's makin' me so mad I could kill him!"

"But you're staying in the office," I pointed out. "Good for you! You won't let Kevin tease you into fighting."

Eddie cocked his head and considered this, then turned back to his folder.

Kevin wrinkled his nose and stuck his tongue out behind Eddie's back. "C'mon Doug. Pull your desk away from the cootie catcher."

"Not now," said Douglas. "It's not that I don't like you or nothin'. I just have to intend to my work."

"You can have my thermos. It's got lemonade," Kevin said.

"Hmmm. You can probably hate me, but no thanks." Douglas buried his face in an upside-down book rather than witness the effect his rejection would have on his friend.

Kevin hadn't quit. "You like these freaks?"

"Twinkle twinkle, little star," came a singsong voice from the closet, "what you *say* is what you *are*."

Kevin flushed.

Douglas looked confused. He couldn't let Julie embarrass Kevin. "Aw shut up. No one asked for your lip!"

I moved toward the closet, expecting Julie to be in tears, but she was running a comb through her auburn hair, and admiring her reflection in a hand mirror.

Kevin glanced at her surreptitiously. "You think you're such a big shot. You think you're so grown up. Wearing nail polish. Carrying a pocketbook with all that junk in it. You think you're so old." He tiptoed to the closet, snatched Julie's purse from the hook, and danced around, holding it out to taunt her.

Julie lost all control. She flew at him, pummeling his shoulders and chest with both fists. She screamed hysterically.

For a moment Kevin was too surprised to react. Then he swung the purse against her cheek. Stunned, she traced the rising welt with her fingertips.

Douglas reached them before me. From behind, he locked both arms around Kevin's waist and dragged him backward. "You've done enough picking on. I hate sissies like you. Girl-picker sissy!"

"Let go of Kevin, please!" I said. "He's to be left alone a while. Sit down, Kevin, and do some thinking. Since you came in this morning, you've tried to provoke everyone but Douglas, and even he's fed up with your teasing and name-calling."

Douglas handed Julie her pocketbook. They both returned to their desks and with a virtuous air opened their folders. Before Julie started to write, she reached in her purse and put on a pair of rhinestone-studded sunglasses.

Kevin sat, but glowered, staring straight ahead.

"You're still angry." I spoke to him privately. "I hope you're angry at the right person."

He answered in a high hollow tone. "Whooo?"

"Yourself. Then perhaps you'll stop causing trouble."

"Noooo," he said.

Eddie worked in isolation until reading time, often the opportunity for confidences. "I'm not supposed to tell you," he began hesitantly. "I was out all night. I stayed under the porch. My mother didn't know I was there."

"She must have worried about you."

"Ha! She didn't even care! One of her boyfriends came over. My sister's so dumb she calls him uncle. I'll never call him uncle!"

"You don't like him to visit your mother."

"They were probably in there kissing." He covered his face with both hands as if to protect himself from the image. "I hate him. Before I left I wrote him a note and put it under my mother's door. I said. 'I hope you die tonight.' Then I ran out."

He paused as if considering his own words. The thought displeased him. Angrily, he shook my arm. "Why did you make me tell? You darn teacher, you! Stop nosing around in my brain!"

"You've had an unhappy night," I said.

"I'd like to kill him. Both of them." Eddie's lips tightened.

One of Mary Quill's third graders, a black boy, was timidly tapping on our door.

"Looking for the teacher? She's at that table." Douglas pointed. "Say how ya doin', kid?"

The boy responded with a fleeting smile and handed me an order form for supplies.

"Thank you," I said.

"Ma'am?"

"Yes?"

"What's wrong with these kids in this class?" The room became absolutely silent. I felt the children waiting. Douglas' chair squeaked. Its front legs rose in the air as he tilted back, arms folded, awaiting my reply.

"What's wrong with these kids?" the child repeated. "Are they here because they don't speak our language?"

I knew the question would someday be asked, but had not yet decided on an answer.

"This class," I found myself saying, "has people in it who need extra help for a little while."

"Yeahhh," Douglas sighed and rocked forward, dropping the front legs of his chair to normal position.

Eddie stood. His voice was shrill. "Are you satisfied, you nosy nigger? Now get outta here!"

Douglas sprang from his seat. He grabbed the messenger by the back of his shirt. The child's eyes bulged, his lips quivered. But Douglas spoke kindly. "Look kid, he gets kinda nervous. He didn't mean it, see?"

Guiding him by the collar, he walked the boy to the hall. On returning, Douglas, teeth clenched, fists ready, headed for Eddie. "I'm sick of keeping you in line, man."

Eddie, still a big talker, cowered under his desk. "What's wrong with that? He's a blackface, you're a blackface." He paused, then added the ultimate insult. "You don't even have a mother or a father."

I was crushed for Douglas, but he didn't need my sympathy. "Listen, you little punk," he shook his index finger, "you don't need a mother or father when you can shave. You've got five more years till you can shave. I've only got four, so you better stop your braggin'."

At noon Julie rewarded Douglas for his earlier gallantry in defending her against Kevin. She offered him her chocolate cupcake.

"You don't hafta gimme this." He stuffed the entire treat in his mouth. "I'd do anything for a lady."

With Douglas and Julie's alliance, Kevin lost his lunch partner and desperately sought another. "Ha! Look at the girl lover, eating with freckle face." He moved his chair to the right, making room for another. "C'mon over to my desk, Jonathan. I'd rather eat with a boy."

Jonathan did not get up. He opened his lunchbox and addressed his reply to a multicolored thermos. His voice quavered. "D—d—don't let him tell me I'm a boy. I'm a ghost. Sometimes I pretend to be a boy, but I'm really a ghost."

Eddie was amused. "Ghosts don't come to school, dummy."

"How could I turn into a boy?" Jonathan's hand trembled as he poured the milk in his thermos cup. "I'm not a magician."

Eddie shrugged and lost interest. He sat with Kevin, and they spent their lunchtime whispering about Douglas and Julie. The would-be victims were too pleased with their own conversation to notice.

"Me and my mother saw you downtown yesterday. What were you doing?" I heard Julie ask Doug.

"Aw, just stealing some stuff."

She looked at him admiringly.

His chest expanded. "I used to wear a disguise, you know. Now they're sure I'm a salesman."

"Gosh, what did you steal?"

"Well . . . nothin'. There's nothin' good in the stores these days."

I sat with Jonathan. "You have a new lunchbox, don't you?" He chomped into a bologna sandwich.

"I see all the boys like spacemen lunchboxes," I said.

"There's no sense telling me that." He took another bite. "I told you I'm a ghost."

"But look, everyone can see you eating and talking and doing fine work. People know that only an intelligent boy can do what you do."

He ate and burped, drank and belched. Despite the ghost talk, and now the long silence, I felt he welcomed my presence.

Finally he stuffed all the used waxed paper back into the lunchbox, wiped his mouth on his sleeve, and spoke without looking up. "You think that's what the world is all about?"

"What do you mean, Jonathan?"

"People with other people?" He played with his fingernails nervously.

"Yes, I think that's what it's all about."

# CHAPTER 20

On a chilly March afternoon Ceil picked me up and we drove to the Child Guidance Center together. On the way I confessed to being nervous about hearing Dr. Bialek's impression of the class and of my teaching. But the meeting went well. To my relief he enthused about what he had observed, commenting on the individualization of instruction, the built-in rewards and consequences, and the value of being able to isolate a child without totally removing him.

His first question concerned Eddie's medication. Having made several appointments with Eddie's mother, which she failed to keep, he wondered whether she was also unreliable about medicating him.

The only pattern I could report with any certainty was a diminishing of the "seizures."

"Have you been in touch with Mrs. Conte?" the doctor asked Ceil.

"Yes, she came to the mothers' group I started last Friday. She never mentioned Eddie, but she told about a new boyfriend and the modeling course she takes three days a week."

"Well, at least she came," Dr. Bialek shrugged. "I'm going to continue him on five milligrams daily, but would you impress on her that I must have periodic checks on the boy?" Hs swiveled his chair in my direction. "It was interesting for me to see the Bergman boy in your group. You know we've been treating the family. A very disturbed child, and frankly I'm pleased he's been able to remain in school. There's one encouraging note. The father has finally gotten involved. He made an appointment to say he noticed some improvement in his son, and now he and Mrs.

Bergman have joined a parents' group here. I originally thought Jonathan might not be able to remain at home, but after seeing him in school, now that the parents are cooperating, I feel more optimistic."

Ceil and I grinned simultaneously. "It's nice to hear good news."

"Mmmm, I'll say."

Ceil looked down at the notes on her lap. "I'd like to discuss Julie. Her mother was very discouraged last Friday. She began talking again about wanting to send her away 'to a school where they keep problem children.' Yet both Mrs. Craig and I feel the girl is progressing."

"She still has a reading problem," I said, "but her difficulties in relating seem more social and much less severe than the other children's."

Dr. Bialek was glancing at Julie's chart. "Let's see, we put her on Tofranil in December. Did the bed-wetting stop?"

Ceil nodded. "Yes. Apparently what's really upsetting Mrs. Neumayer now is that Julie constantly challenges her about being adopted. She often says, 'I hate you. My real mother would be nice to me. She wouldn't be mean like you'."

"I think it's interesting," Dr. Bialek leaned back in his leather chair, "that we see ten times as many adopted children in clinics than their proportional number in the population. Time and again these children are troubled with the very thoughts Julie is expressing. While the original parent is idealized, the adoptive parent becomes the scapegoat.

"As in Julie's case, learning problems are not uncommon. This girl does not have a brain dysfunction, but the adopted child's ability to learn may be hampered by the great amount of energy he invests in the longing for, the hopeless unfulfilled search for, his natural parents. At the same time he may unwittingly be holding back because he has unconsciously confused learning with learning about adoption.

"I have approached adoption agencies about better ways for the situation to be handled, but until changes are effected it's our job to help parents understand that some complications are not abnormal for the adopted child. It's a major step for parents to accept this."

Dr. Bialek rubbed his ear thoughtfully. "What about these parents?" he asked.

"I've been seeing Julie's mother weekly," Ceil said, "but I feel we've just arrived at the crux of the problem. Julie's about at the same stage. Just beginning to deal with what adoption means to her."

The psychiatrist pointed his index finger at Ceil. "Ah, but that's the important thing!"

We knew he had another appointment in five minutes, so at Ceil's request I summarized recent developments with Douglas and Kevin, including Julie's observation that Douglas was getting "better" while Kevin was "worser."

Dr. Bialek rose. "There's little I can add to that. It proves that therapy is not confined to a clinic. You and these children have established a therapeutic community." He shook hands with each of us. "I only hope there'll be more classes soon."

"What does he mean, 'better ways to handle adoption'?" I asked Ceil as we drove back to school.

"I've heard him on the subject before," she said. "He feels the current practice of repeating to the young child over and over again the story of his adoption undermines his establishing his identity as a person. It's much better, he thinks, to have the child grow up without this burden. Because the information won't have affected his early development, he'll be better able to cope with it later."

"Isn't the big concern that a child might find out accidentally?"

"Yes, but he believes it's worth that risk, because the older the child, the better. It would be traumatic, of course, but a single trauma. Less damaging than the day-by-day effect on the younger child who fantasizes for years about missing parents and resists those he lives with."

# CHAPTER 21

The morning after our conference with Dr. Bialek, Eddie was in trouble before he entered the room.

Julie came running in and threw herself at me. "Mrs. Craig," she was breathless, "Eddie's been saying awful things to me on the bus."

"Do you want to tell me?"

"No, I can't," she said. "It's so bad. He said two swear words! He said

Julie, Julie, little fool-y
How does your farting go?
With silver bells and cockleshells
And pretty maids all in a row.

She seemed to enjoy repeating it, and I was curious. "Two swear words?"

"Yes! Farting and cockle. You've got to stop him!"

In came the swearer. He sat on the floor, pulled off his boots, and hurled them into the closet. I started to reprimand him for this when he suddenly clutched his hand to his throat. He looked frightened, and gasped. Then like a two-year-old in tantrum, he turned and lay on his stomach, his arms and legs flailing.

"Eddie!" I had to shout above his noises. "That doesn't mean anything! If something's wrong, you have to say it!"

With a thud his head struck the floor. His eyes were closed, arms and body motionless.

"You know you don't have to do this." I grasped his forearm. "When there's a problem, we talk about it. It won't be solved this way."

"What's a matter, punk, lose your key?" Douglas' voice was taunting. It hit home.

Eddie sprang up and pounced on him, pounding his chest and kicking his shins. "You took it! You took it! That's how you know. Oh, oh, I'll be locked out!"

Douglas, unprepared for the attack, received the blows without retaliating.

"Where'd you put it?" Eddie was more frantic each second. He seized the front of Douglas' shirt. A button popped into the air.

"That does it," Douglas growled through clenched teeth. "I'll never tell ya."

"I knew it!" Eddie hopped around, pointing his arm at Douglas. "I knew that black boog took it!"

Douglas, incredibly cool, turned away, and strolled to his seat. "You're not getting me in trouble, punk."

I planted both hands firmly on Eddie's bony shoulders and with little resistance directed him to his chair.

Kevin, Julie and Jonathan, who had been cowering in the closet, took advantage of the lull to scurry to their desks.

"When you're ready and through with name-calling, we'll talk about your key." I stayed behind Eddie, close enough to move if he should rise.

"I'm ready! I'm ready!" His voice was shrill, his face tense. "My mother's at her beauty school. I'm supposed to let myself in. I put the key on a string around my neck. Somebody musta untied it on the bus. Now I'm locked out! She won't be home till seven-thirty!"

"Doug." I stood in front of him. He was nearly as tall as I. His arms were folded across his chest, his eyes blank. "You had wonderful control, not losing your temper, when he tried so hard to make you. You see how upset Eddie is to have lost the key. Do you know anything about it?"

He shrugged innocently.

"You admitted it!" Eddie yelled. "You said you'd never tell."

"Because you made me mad." Douglas' nostrils were flaring, his temper rising.

"Did you see it, Doug?" I had gone too far.

"Oh, don't believe me, huh? Okay, lieutenant, search." He

kicked off his sneakers, peeled off each sock, stood barefoot and faced the wall, holding his hands above his head. "Aren't ya gonna frisk me?"

"I don't want to—"

"Think I have it, ha?" He whipped his belt from its loops and started to undo his pants. "C'mon, lieutenant, tell me where I put it."

Eddie leaped from his chair and tore across the room. He pummeled Douglas on the back before he had a chance to turn around. "I can't stand people who do things to me! I'll get you for this!"

Douglas wheeled to face his assailant and punched him in the stomach. Eddie doubled over, with a piercing cry.

I got between them, but Eddie darted around me to kick Douglas in the shin. Douglas got his arm around the smaller boy's waist and flipped him. They tumbled across the room, punching as they rolled.

From the corner of my eye, I glimpsed the other children. Jonathan had the cover of his desk up and his head inside. Julie trembled. Kevin, stamping his feet, shouted, "Get him, Doug! Kill the punk!"

"You bastard punk." Doug was now on top of Eddie, and socked him in the nose.

I reached the itnercom. "Doris? Eleanor. I need help, quick!"

"You boog," Eddie screamed. "I'm gonna kill you." And he writhed away from Douglas long enough to jump up and grab a chair. He held it upside down, over his head, ready to swing. Douglas was just getting to his feet.

I knew the chair could fracture Doug's skull, but there was no way to stop Eddie in time. I dug my hands under Doug's arms to drag him out of range just as Eddie released the chair. It dropped a foot short of its mark, so forcefully that two legs caved in.

Douglas fought my grip. "Let go, let go of me!"

Miss Silverstein rushed in, with the nurse, Mrs. Rogers, a few steps behind.

Quickly sizing things up, they backed Eddie into a corner. Both women held his arms, but with enormous strength the small boy twisted his whole body forward in a convulsive, jerking motion until he was free. "Keep your dirty hands off me! I hate your guts!" He headed for Douglas. I released Douglas, hoping to catch Eddie. But he darted through the kneehole of my desk. Douglas and he quickly locked in another struggle.

Arms around each other, they landed together on the floor, first Eddie on top, then Douglas. I grabbed the back of Doug's pants, loosened because he had removed the belt. Miss Silverstein and the nurse had reached us. Douglas fell off Eddie and collapsed beside him, with a deep agonized moan. Blood was seeping through the shoulder of his blue shirt.

Eddie, terrified at the sight, crawled under my desk and sat huddled, his knees to his chin. "I'm sorry, I'm sorry!" he cried.

Flushed but efficient, the nurse undid Doug's shirt and gently eased it away from his shoulder, to expose the wound.

Blood gushed from at least ten separate punctures. Eddie's upper and lower teeth had penetrated deeply into Douglas' flesh.

"Help," Douglas said feebly.

"You'll be all right," she assured him. "Rest a minute. Then we'll go to my office and fix you."

"Help," his voice was stronger now. "I've got that little punk's germs in me."

"Come on now." The nurse supported the heavy boy. "Let's get antiseptic on it."

He leaned his body against hers, his head on her shoulder. He shut his eyes and extended his hands as if groping blindly. Slowly, she led him out.

"I could have blood poisoning," his voice rang through the hall, "from that little punk's mouth!"

Kevin's feet vigorously protested his friend's injury. Tap-tap, heel-toe. Julie gnawed the back of her hand. Jonathan turned his atomic radiator on each of us. "K-yew! Pow-pow!"

Like mirror images, Miss Silverstein and I looked at one another and shook our heads.

I stooped beside my desk. Eddie was shivering. "Let me help you. I know you're upset."

He shifted in the cramped area, turning his back to me.

Miss Silverstein spoke gently. "Come and have a talk, Eddie."

Anything would have triggered him. "Gimme one good reason

why I should!" He leaped up. "I hate principals like you. I hate this whole stinkin' place! I've been in trouble in every school I've ever been in."

"You could help yourself, you know. You don't have to be in trouble," she said.

"Ha-ha," he sneered.

He wrapped his hand around the heavy stapler on my blotter and hurled it at the principal, barely missing her head. Next he threw a workbook at Kevin's chest. "Shut up your goddamn feet!" Then a barrage of books, pencils, and rulers flew through the air. "Bitches, fucking bastards!" he repeated. A book struck my hip as I approached him. A box of crayons broke open in mid-air. Some hit Julie, and she began to cry.

With his ammunition gone, Eddie gripped the back of my chair, rested his right knee on the seat, and used his left foot to pump, like a scooter. The free-wheeling casters responded. Riding it, he propelled my chair first against Kevin's desk, then Jonathan's.

Miss Silverstein and I caught him on the rebound. Purple-faced, he screamed profanities and tried to bite our restraining hands. He struggled briefly, got away, and charged at Julie. "I hate crybabies!" He yanked her hair.

This time we locked Eddie's hands behind him, lifted him by the elbow, and rushed down the hall. His feet didn't hit the floor till we reached the main office.

"Would you give us a hand?" Miss Silverstein directed her gaping secretary. "Mrs. Craig has to get back."

Mrs. Rogers met me in the classroom. "Douglas may need tetanus. I'll drive him home and ask the grandmother the date of his last shot. If necessary I'll take them to the hospital. Let me have his things. He won't be back today."

There were a few moments of shuffling, then Douglas' fading voice. "I still feel his germs! You gotta test that punk for rabies!"

No word of Eddie for another hour. Julie put on earphones and did a taped lesson, Kevin used the controlled reader, and I taught Jonathan short division. "A ghost doin' numbers? Oooo . . . eeee! You gotta be crazy!" But in spite of his fantasies, he learned very quickly.

At twelve, Doris sauntered in. "Mrs. Conte's in the office. Miss

Silverstein wants you to talk to her. I'm supposed to stay here."

"Ya? Well, what'd the other kid do to him?" Eddie's mother was pointing her cigarette at Miss Silverstein when I entered the office. "That's what I wanna know."

The principal indicated with a nod that I was to sit between them. There were other chairs around her desk, but Eddie stood against the wall, fearfully watching his mother.

Miss Silverstein said, "Mrs. Craig could tell you what happened from the beginning."

While I described Eddie's morning, he kept his hands over his ears. Yet he winced when I told about his biting. "The key was part of his upset, Mrs. Conte, but he had been teasing on the bus before he lost it. Would you know if something else might be bothering him?"

"I'm upset too, getting called out of my classes to come for him. I paid for those classes. I'm supposed to be in makeup right now." Her eyes were beaded with mascara, her brows plucked thin and penciled in.

"Sometimes children his age are afraid of going home to an empty house. Is there someone he could be with after school?" I asked.

"Listen, I got my daughter over at my girl friend's, but she's not gonna take two of them." She jerked her thumb in Eddie's direction. "How long's he suspended for?"

"Two days. From now until Friday," Miss Silverstein said. "When he comes back, we hope he'll be ready to stay with no more interruptions."

"He'll be ready all right. I'll beat him till he's ready." Eddie began to whimper.

"That won't help him learn to control himself." I couldn't conceal my anger.

"It better!" she got up. "I'm not missing more classes for him. My kids don't have a ball and chain on me."

As she dragged Eddie out, his whimpering developed into full-scale crying.

# CHAPTER 22

"I had a disturbing conversation yesterday," Ceil was saying before school on Friday. "Just as I was leaving the office, Eddie's mother called.

"She'd locked him in his room for the day and gone to modeling school. A policeman was waiting inside when she got home. One of the neighbors had seen Eddie climb out his bedroom window onto the roof. Afraid he'd fall, she called the police. But he just stood there exposing himself. The officer said he wouldn't file a juvenile report, but threatened Mrs. Conte with child-abuse charges if she locked him up again. Can you believe, she doesn't see anything wrong with that? She's just furious at the boy for getting her in trouble."

"Oh God, that's so discouraging," Ceil," I said. I was facing the window. The bus had turned into the driveway.

"I thought about him for hours." Ceil picked up her briefcase. "At least we know, now, more of what's going on. Maybe we'll have to face an unpleasant decision. As long as he's in that home, Eddie may never be better."

"They're here." I heard the door open. "What's your schedule?"

"Send him in at nine. I'd like to see him first."

"Okay. I'm anxious to talk to you after school," I said.

"Right, but we'll have to cut it short. Don't forget the reception for our new boss at four in the Administration Building. Have a good day."

Seeing Eddie come down the hall, I knew his two-day absence had served no purpose. Rather than helping him understand that disruptive behavior was unacceptable, it had increased his need to act out. We had to find an alternative to exclusion for children whose problems were aggravated at home.

Eddie was already provoking Douglas, crisscrossing in front of him, impeding his progress. "I'll bite you anytime I want! My teeth are good weapons. I bite my sister, too."

"Use them again and you'll be swallowing them." Douglas held up his lunchbox menacingly. They stopped, ready to fight, a few feet from our room.

"Good morning, Doug," I called. "Take a look at the new puzzle on your desk." Hand on his back, I guided him in. "And Eddie, I'm glad you're back." I directed him straight ahead with the other hand. "Mrs. Black wants to see you first today."

While Eddie was with Ceil, the rest of the class did creative writing. More and more, our mornings were passing peacefully and productively. Even rewards, stars, prizes, and privileges were less urgently sought. The feeling of success, the satisfaction when work was well done, was becoming a goal in itself.

But Eddie's return an hour later interrupted the day's progress. "You're not telling me what to do! I'm not sitting down!" he yelled as he jogged in.

"You're standing up?" I said.

"That's right! So would you if you got whipped like me. I hate getting whipped. It doesn't do any good. I'll just do it all over. Next time I get locked in I'm gonna make a bomb. I'll blow up the stinkin' house. Then I'll get out."

"Whoo-ee! You'll get out in a hundred pieces!" Jonathan now was much more aware of the other children. Though he had not yet learned to converse, he made occasional comments.

"Here's your folder." I handed it to Eddie. "Where are you going to stand?"

With a red crayon he scrawled "fuck you" across the cover.

"Psst!" Kevin stage-whispered to Douglas. "What'd your grandmother say about that mad dog bitin' you?"

Eddie turned pale. He clutched the folder to his chest and watched Douglas anxiously.

"I wouldn't tell who did it." Douglas rubbed his bandaged wound. "I may be mean, but I'm not that mean."

Eddie sagged with relief. He looked around, headed for the

windowsill, placed his folder there and opened it. He stood as he wrote. After a brief silence, he turned toward the group. "Hey Doug, wanna have a race? See who's done first?"

"I would've, but you've been takin' too much sweat out on me. It's just 'cause you hate dark skin, right?"

"Naw! It's 'cause I didn't used t' like ya. But now I do."

"Okay," said Doug cautiously. "Ready, get set, go!"

Kevin was irked at being excluded from the competition.

"Let's hide the punk's lunch," he said to Douglas.

"No thanks." Douglas kept working.

Within an hour he was raising his fist in a victorious gesture. "I'm winning! I'm winning!"

From Eddie's vantage at the window he could see that Douglas' last assignment, tracing the human body from his science book, was almost completed.

Eddie threw his pencil down. His voice was high-pitched, whiny. "You big bragger! Just because I don't feel like bragging!"

Too pleased with himself to be offended, Douglas said, "I'm sorry, I was conscientious of braggin'."

Julie handed Eddie his pencil, which had rolled under her chair. As if pleading his case, he said to her. "He's makin' me nervous! It's not nice to brag, ya know."

"You're doin' good, Eddie." Julie glanced at his work and returned to her own, cutting sandpaper versions of those trouble-some letters b, p, and d.

Then Douglas, with a side glance at Eddie, shouted with enthusiasm, "I'm losing! I'm losing!"

"Liar! You liar!" Eddie threw his papers and books across the room. "You know you were winning!"

"Think, Eddie." I stayed beside Jonathan, hoping the incident would go no further. "Why would Douglas say he was losing?"

"Because I've got manners," Douglas interposed. With both hands in the pockets of his ragged jeans, he walked confidently toward the window. "Just take five minutes off, Mrs. Craig. I can handle this."

"Thanks, anyway," I said. "Only one teacher to a room."

Forgetting his sore bottom, Eddie boosted himself onto the windowsill, away from Douglas, who was addressing him. "You better start respecting your elders, kid. I say I'm losing, I'm losing. Don't forget who's already nine."

Feeling threatened, Eddie knew only one response. He crouched, readying himself to jump down on Douglas.

"If you say you lost, Doug," I spoke loudly, "that means Eddie gets first choice for the afternoon.

"I take woodworking." Eddie abandoned the attack.

"Uh-uh," Kevin muttered under his breath. "That's what I choose."

"S-S-S. Pow-pow." Jonathan rocked back and forth in his seat.

"We use words, Jonathan. Remember?" I said. "What's the trouble?"

"I don't know any word beginning with S. Pow-pow." He held up the anagram.

"Easy." Douglas turned away from Eddie. "Psychological. Like disturbed children. And it's psychological how black people and white people treat each other. Don't ya hear the S?"

Jonathan rummaged through a mound of letters and produced S-I-K-O-L-O.

"Still," Douglas looked out the window, "white people might get black themselves if they stayed in the sun too long."

Julie was listening thoughtfully. "Or a beautiful brown like you," she said.

"Gee, thanks. I never heard such a complimentary thing about my skin." He lifted his desktop and poked through the contents. "How about havin' my eraser?"

Julie didn't reach for it. "Maybe my mother would like it." Her eyes were downcast. "She's mad at me, but I'm not not sure why."

"Why don't you think about yourself?" He tossed it on her desk.

"I don't like to." She toyed with the eraser. "It makes me feel sad."

Kevin nodded. "Me too," he said softly.

She smiled at him. "You're like me."

The blush began at his neck and spread to the roots of his hair.

Eddie slid off the windowsill, pointing at the embarrassed boy. He danced around his desk. "Ha-ha! Look! Kevin's havin' an orgy!"

Douglas pounded his desk. "That does it!" He jumped up. "Didn't I say respect your elders?"

"Wha'd I do?" Eddie backed away.

"You teased." Julie rose to join Douglas.

"Yah!" Douglas was closing in.

"Boo!" said Jonathan from his desk.

Kevin, shielded by Douglas and Julie, sneered, "Mad dog. Biter."

Eddie went wild. He dashed by Julie and out the door and collided with a small girl, knocking her down. "Whad're you lookin' at, you bugger?" He ran into the bathroom.

"Who wants to see my pisser?" We heard him yell. To the horror of two innocent occupants, who fled, I entered the boys' bathroom.

Eddie had already flooded one of three sinks, by jamming the drain with wadded toilet paper.

"Get outta here!" he said. "I'm gonna have a BM."

"You're blocking the sink," I said. "I'm not letting you get in trouble today. Let's go."

"Back to the nut room? Where everybody hates me?"

"To our room or to the principal." I turned off the water. He ran ahead and was in his seat when I got there.

In spite of the morning, lunchtime was peaceful. Eddie, in fact, tolerated a brief discussion about why no one liked him.

"You start fights."

"You bit Douglas."

"And you always swear."

This was the only charge he answered. "My mother swears at me. Why can't I swear too?"

For afternoon play, Douglas chose the truck and Julie the loom. Jonathan painted at the easel. Eddie hammered two pieces of wood together, fashioning a sword.

But Kevin could not play. He was still procrastinating over his morning assignments.

I was correcting workbooks when Julie suddenly jingled a shiny object. "Look what I found in the yarn box!" The lost key.

Eddie dropped the hammer. "That proves it! Someone hid it. Who did it? I knew someone stole it."

He twisted Julie's wrist. The key fell. "Oh! Don't."

"Was it you? Was it?"

"I just found it. Help! Let go!"

Douglas headed for Eddie. I stepped between them and ushered Eddie to the isolated "office." "Then it was Douglas or Kevin," he yelled on the way. "Jonathan wouldn't."

"Ghosts don't use keys," said Jonathan. He continued at the easel, smearing another paper with globs of brown paint. "We go through keyholes."

"You're a harsh kid," said Douglas and shook his fist toward Eddie. "Watch who you're accusin'."

Kevin sat back, smiling smugly, his arms folded across his chest. Then, realizing I was watching him, he lowered his head. The tapping began. Heel-toe. Heel-toe.

"Shut up your feet!" Eddie blocked his ears.

"We're taking a few minutes right now," I said, "to discuss the key. Someone knows how it got in the box. That person's caused a lot of trouble."

"Listen, judge. Everybody wanted to get that punk. We're all guilty, okay?" Douglas faced me, hands on hips, his chin thrust out pugnaciously.

"Do you all agree with that?" I turned to the others.

"He's asked for it," said Julie.

"Yeah," Kevin whispered.

"Ooo-ooo," moaned Jonathan.

"Asked for what?" I was angry. "When someone's got a problem, he needs your help. I thought that's what we were here for. You've all been upset one time or another. Would you like being teased about something important to you? Yet you admit wanting to contribute to his unhappiness. I agree. You're all guilty. It's not my idea of why we've come together."

There was a long silence. Julie hung her head. Kevin scuffed his shoes. Jonathan painted his left hand brown. Eddie sat rigidly facing the wall.

Finally, Douglas cleared his throat. "Please God," he folded his hands, "will she always be a softy?" But he picked up the key, shuffled over to Eddie, and left it on his desk.

"Thanks, Doug."

Eddie didn't turn. He sounded choked.

"Can Eddie play now, Mrs. Craig?" Julie asked.

"Are you ready to play without fighting, Eddie? Has this helped you understand what you do to make people angry?"

The activities were resumed. Kevin rejected my offer of help. "Why should I finish? I can't get the workbench anyhow."

"That's just an excuse, Kevin. You hadn't even started when Eddie chose woodworking."

I went back to the workbooks and didn't notice Kevin walk to the closet. Then Eddie yelled, "No ya don't!"

Kevin had Eddie's jacket, holding it by the label and dangling it out the window, just as Douglas had done with his sweater seven months before. When Eddie approached the window, Kevin let go. It caught on a bush, a few feet off the ground.

"My mother'll kill me!" Eddie ran to the outside exit.

Expressionless, Kevin leaned out to watch.

Douglas, playing on the floor, looked up from the cardboard garage he was constructing. "Will wonders never cease," he said. "Why don't you control it, Kevin? You're startin' to act bad like me, and I'm startin' to act good like you."

"Luckily the bus came while Eddie was getting his jacket," I told Ceil, as we sat over coffee in the teacher's lounge. "I don't know what he'd have done to Kevin if there'd been more time."

"You really had a day." But her smile vanished quickly. "I've been thinking about Eddie. He's no better, El, and I'm not getting anywhere with him or his mother. He's in trouble in school, at home, and in the community.

"I heard from the police. The woman upstairs has been calling the station to say the kids are often alone all night. Wednesday evening she called again. She'd heard the little girl screaming and went to check. The sister told her that Eddie had been playing with matches and set a curtain on fire. He managed to pull it down and douse the flames. The woman came and asked to see Eddie. He appeared at the door with a butcher knife and told her to mind her own business, not quite that politely."

"You're leading up to something," I said.

She paused to sip the coffee. "I wish I felt more hopeful. It might be different if his mother would cooperate. She's stopped coming to group. Won't see me or Dr. Bialek at all. I finally reached her by phone today. She was high on something, talking strangely and breathing heavily.

"The lieutenant who called won't institute legal action if we make some other recommendation. If it should go to court, it's possible that the judge's only alternative might be to place him in a foster home. Knowing his current state, he wouldn't last a month with foster parents."

Another long pause. "Ceil, what do you think."

"He's crying for help. More help than we can give. We should consider residential treatment for Eddie."

I wasn't surprised, nor did I want to burden her with my feeling of failure. "Where?"

"Green Valley is nearest, but I'll have to check on their intake. We have vacation the second week in April. Would you want to see a few possibilities with me?"

We agreed to visit wherever openings existed. Meanwhile, we would present Eddie's case to the Transitional Class Committee for review, inviting Dr. Bialek to attend, and ask for recommendations. Any plan, of course, would have to be accepted by Eddie's mother.

# CHAPTER 23

The only date available for the conference was the Friday before April vacation. Mr. Hanley sent a memo asking that we all arrive early to meet his new assistant, Mr. Jerome Brenner. Since his responsibility would be nonretarded special education, Mr. Brenner was my new boss.

Containers of coffee and a trayful of cookies were provided for the occasion. Mr. Hanley, a genuinely warm, outgoing man, made the introductions.

Our new boss, Mr. Brenner stood about six-feet-four and was handsome in a boyish way, with jet black locks cascading over his forehead, deep-set blue eyes, high cheek bones, and cavernous dimples on both sides of his wide mouth. His handshake was more like a workout.

Fifteen minutes of small talk and the meeting was called to order. The committee now consisted of ten. Mr. Brenner opened by requesting more information in writing, specific diagnoses, goals, and statistical data. We had invested so much in this program, I was surprised he would think we were light on paperwork.

"May we hear from Mrs. Craig first?"

I was summarizing Eddie's behavior and academic performance from the time he joined us in November.

"Mrs. Craig," Mr. Brenner interrupted, "exactly what are the transient symptomatic manifestations of such a child? Is this obsessive compulsive reaction?"

"I'm afraid I can only speak as his teacher, Mr. Brenner. Dr. Bialek does the psychiatric evaluation."

He slouched in his chair, impatiently tapping a pencil against his teeth until I finished.

Ceil described her private sessions with Eddie, and her contacts with his mother. She too was interrupted.

"I'm going to see this woman." Mr. Brenner pointed the pencil at Ceil. "I've dealt with this kind of parent before. She does all her thinking between her legs."

Miss Silverstein gasped. Mr. Hanley coughed. Ceil's eyebrows shot up. We exchanged quick glances.

"Flattery will throw her off balance," he continued. "It's a technique insecure persons can't handle. They fall apart. When her defenses are down, she'll willingly accept help."

The door opened slowly. A junior high school counselor, trying not to attract attention, slipped into the one vacant chair around the large oak table. "Sorry," she murmured, "we had bus problems."

Mr. Hanley introduced Mr. Brenner, who offered the vigorous handshake.

"Say," grinned the counselor. "You must've chosen that tie to match your eyes. I've never seen anyone's eyes look more blue!"

Mr. Brenner blushed instantly. He clutched his tie, stammered, cleared his throat, and sat down looking uncomfortable.

Miss Silverstein winked at me. It was hard not to laugh.

Dr. Bialek reviewed psychiatric information, including test results. "If this mother had been more reliable," he added, "medication might have helped. When the boy annoyed her, she gave him twice as much, other days nothing, so I stopped the prescription."

"Thank you, Doctor." Mr. Hanley then outlined possible plans for Eddie, including foster placement and residential treatment. "Has anyone other suggestions?"

Mr. Brenner, still looking embarrassed, said nothing.

Miss Silverstein referred to her note pad. "It seems to me, only one course offers all this child requires: therapy, a school plan, full-time care, and help from people who have experience with his kind of need."

The discussion continued for an hour before it was unanimous that the committee would recommend residential treatment for Eddie.

"Then Mrs. Black and Mrs. Craig will report again after they visit these places." Mr. Hanley rose. "Beyond that, we can't do anything till we get the mother's consent.

"Leave that to me," said Mr. Brenner.

I thought it would be nice to begin Easter vacation with a ravioli dinner.

"You know I hate cheese-filled ravioli," Ann complained. "I only like the meat kind."

"Cheese is best," Richie declared with his mouth full.

"Who asked you? And stop eating till we've all been served!" Ann grabbed the fork from Richie's hand, provoking a roar of protest.

I dropped the ladle onto the platter, splattering Ellen and myself with tomato sauce. "Stop it! Stop it this minute! I can't stand this arguing!" I was usually able to ignore this kind of bickering, but tonight it was shattering. Bill and the kids stared at me while I wiped Ellen's face, then my own with my apron. The soft calico was so soothing on my eyes that I wanted to weep into it—without really knowing why.

Stony silence prevailed as we ate. But as food so often lulled my class, it now worked magically on my family and me. Bill opened a bottle of wine and, urged by the boys, was soon regaling us for the thousandth time with the story of his unsuccessful major league tryout many years ago. "I'll tell you this, kids. There's nothing I wouldn't give to put on that Red Sox uniform just once."

I don't know whether it was the wine or the story that went to my head, but I chuckled, then couldn't stop laughing.

"What's so funny, Mom?" Richie put his hand on my arm.

"She's cracking up," Ann said.

"No, no," I finally gasped, "I'm just admiring your blue eyes. All five sets."

# CHAPTER 24

There were only two facilities in our state that might be available to Eddie. Neither expected an opening before July. Thursday morning of vacation week was bright and warm. I picked Ceil up at eight, and we set out to visit both schools.

The first was state-run, Green Valley Center, about an hour's drive from my home. It offered residence, treatment, and education to fifty boys from six to sixteen.

A tall cyclone fence surrounded the entire property. Ceil and I expressed the same initial disappointment as we waited for the watchman to unlock the gate and admit my car. There were five brick buildings on as many acres, separated by sparsely equipped playgrounds and athletic fields. Designed for economy, the place looked sterile and unpromising.

A black male social worker took us first to his office. He had received Eddie's record, and we discussed his case and the program at Green Valley.

"We've been operating nine years," he said, lighting a cigarette. "It took us four to develop the group controls that make our school a success. A child like Eddie quickly learns that misbehavior will get him confined to the 'house,' as we call our main building. If that's not enough, we use room restriction and, in extreme cases, bed restriction, with a staff member placed outside the child's room.

"Our goal is to get them back home. Occasionally, a child is so badly off we ship him to the state hospital. Others need foster placement, but most go home. Of course, that means we work intensively with the family. We wouldn't take the boy without some assurance his mother will cooperate."

Ceil and I exchanged glances.

"When a child begins improving, he earns short home visits. Before he returns for good, these extend to weekends and longer, until we're sure as possible he's ready to remain. About one in five comes back, but the second stay is usually briefer."

He took us through the main floor. "You'll see those on house restriction today." There were four children in the recreation room. A boy about seven chewed on the head of a rubber doll, then banged it against the floor. "Do you? Do you understand? Do you?" He pushed the doll's eyes in.

An older boy sat on the floor, masturbating as he stared vacantly. Two teen-agers, back to back in lounge chairs, exchanged profanities.

"You here again, John?" the social worker asked one of them. "Better stay in class tomorrow."

Two shiny-haired girls in blue jeans moved among the children. "Trainees from Teachers College," our guide said "They're here in shifts twenty-four hours a day, watching the ones on restriction, planning after-school activities, even sitting up with a kid who's had a nightmare. We wouldn't be able to function without them."

To make the most of our visit, we had agreed in advance to observe in different classes. Ceil went to the middle group. I chose the youngest, ten children, six to eight years old. They sat at battered desks in a dreary green room. Paint peeled near the ceiling and baseboards.

The boys looked in need of mothers, to fuss about combing hair, washing necks, and choosing matching clothes. They were a ragged bunch but sat at attention, eyes riveted on the male teacher, who continued scolding a boy at the board for making numbers carelessly.

When a thin redhead reached stealthily into his desk, the teacher turned. "Boyle! I've told you to keep your hands on your desk!" Grabbing the back of his pants, the teacher yanked Boyle from his chair. He pointed to the clock. "You've got two minutes to be up at the house, or else."

After assigning the others a page of seatwork, he walked to the back of the room where I sat observing.

"I understand you're in special ed." He drew up a small chair and sat on it backward, leaning toward me. "Any questions?"

"Yes, about the discipline."

"Rigid, eh?" He seemed pleased. "That's why we don't believe in women teachers. Even classroom aides are male. What woman's gonna hold a kid by the pants till his crotch hurts?"

"Is it always this structured?" I resisted the temptation to challenge his male arrogance.

"You bet," he nodded. "And because it is we're forcing achievement from kids for the first time in their lives."

I looked around. Every boy was bent over his paper in the silent room.

"What's the average stay?" I asked.

"Most are here two years, but it's flexible. When a kid seems ready, we try him in a local public school at least a few months before sending him home. I sometimes use the public school to shake up a kid who won't cooperate here. That's enough to make him want to learn."

"Bartlett, collect the papers," he barked and returned to the front of the room.

After a grammar lesson, there was a break for juice and cookies. The boys were allowed to walk in the corridor.

Hearing whispering, the teacher and I looked out. A frail dark-haired boy had been cornered in the hall by two youngsters who barely reached his shoulder. They took turns swinging green cloth book bags, repeatedly striking the taller boy. He made no effort to resist or even protect himself.

"Mr. Jackson, Mr. Jackson," he said pitifully. "They're doing it again."

The teacher shrugged. "Too bad you let them, Charlie." He walked back in the classroom.

If I hadn't looked shocked, I doubt that he would have referred to the incident. "That boy wants to die," he jerked his thumb toward the victim, "but he expects someone else to do it for him."

Ceil's experience was similar, though she felt none of my agitation about the male teacher requirement. "They have a point with the kind of kids they get," she said, "especially since most of the dorm aides are women."

During the twenty-mile drive to Kirby School, near the state capital, we tried to project how Eddie might fare at Green Valley.

"The teacher seemed sadistic to me," I said, "doing nothing while a child was beaten. And I see no advantage for the two who virtually had permission to be cruel."

"Still, it's hard to judge an isolated incident," Ceil said. "Each of those children is in treatment, and the teacher meets daily with the therapist. It's paradise compared to some state schools I've visited. We may not see better."

But Kirby School looked much better. We found the name on the gatehouse of what must have been an enormous private estate. The tree-lined road to the main house curved past beautifully tended lawns, tennis courts, and a lovely pond. The building was a gracious mansion fronted with marble columns.

Miss Kirby, the director, greeted us. She was a tiny dynamic woman about fifty. He father, a psychologist, had founded the school. "We're a private institution, you know, drawing children from seventeen states. They stay year round. In the summer we run a camp." She spoke over her shoulder as she led us through the marble foyer and one carpeted room after another.

"This is Peter." She stopped by a heavy-set youth who was vacuuming the oriental rug. "He's been with us eighteen years, haven't you dear?"

Peter smiled broadly.

"Many of our students remain on in adulthood."

We followed her into an impressive paneled office, furnished in Danish modern.

"Please sit down. I read your little fellow's record." She looked directly at me and smiled sympathetically. "Such a tragic story."

"But Eddie has a lot going for him, Miss Kirby," I replied. "He's really bright, you know. What he's had to contend with might well have been more damaging to another child. We think if Eddie could get away from home, and receive treatment, he should have a good chance."

I sat back, wondering what Ceil thought of my sudden optimism.

"Well, yes." Miss Kirby's smile wavered. "And we believe you've come to the right place. Our psychologist and teachers tailor a program for each child's needs."

"And do you work with parents?" Ceil asked.

"Well, of course we rarely see them, but many take the children at Christmas time. We do send bimonthly reports to each family. And we have some fine families." Her voice warmed. "The son of our congressional representative is here, and the daughter of a well-known composer has been with us four years."

"I'll show you the nursery before the children nap." We followed a flagstone path to the one-story white frame structure, housing that group alone.

The six boys and two girls in the beautifully equipped room were supervised by two young teachers. One child assumed an all-too-familiar position, face down, flat on the floor. A mongoloid boy about four sat in a stroller, which one of the teachers gently rocked. A handsome blond paced restlessly, constantly shaking his hands as if they had been immersed in water and he sought to rid himself of the excess. The other teacher squatted by a large girl, who lay on a chenille bath mat and sucked a nursing bottle. Suddenly she stiffened and let out a piercing scream, then relaxed and returned to the bottle. Minutes later, she screamed again.

We heard her periodic cries from a distance as we toured three other units. The group Eddie's age sat isolated from one another in an orderly room. Each boy wore a jacket and tie. The plump matronly teacher moved from desk to desk.

"What's your word today, Sarah?" She put her arm around a child about ten, the only girl in the group. A magic-markered word card was taped to her desk. She clutched the teacher's hand. "Jump?" The blonde child smiled radiantly. "Play?"

"No, Sarah, it's run—R-U-N."

"Run?" Sarah's smile remained unchanged.

Miss Kirby brought us to the oldest group last. Eleven well-dressed boys, ranging in age from fourteen to nineteen, all doing math. One worked from a geometry book; another struggled to count heads. A heavy-set youth, badly in need of a shave, raised his hand. He spoke as if each word were an effort. "I—have—to—go—to—the—bat—room."

There was every sort of handicapped child: retarded, brain damaged, and emotionally disturbed. Could it be where Eddie belonged? Green Valley had seemed so severe. Was it a better choice than this beautiful sheltered place?

# CHAPTER 25

We returned to school on Monday, April twenty-fourth.

My parade of before-school visitors, I was now sure, were good candidates for Ceil's casework if not for Transitional Class.

"Those finks on my road," Paul whined as he washed the blackboard. "All vacation they called me names. David punched me, so I kicked him back, but his father saw only what I did and told me to stay away. It really hurt when he punched."

He rested the sponge on the chalk tray and leaned on a desk near mine. "Do you like David?" he asked.

"I don't even know him," I smiled. "But I don't like to hear he punched you."

After a short silence, he said, "If you saw him, what would you do?"

"What would you want me to do?"

"I don't know." But his eyes searched mine. I had to find the right answer.

"Would you want me to say he should never hurt you again?"

"Oh no, don't say that." Paul picked up his books. "Cause he'll never be my friend if you do."

Sharon waited until Paul's footsteps had faded. "Know what happen?" Her black pigtails bobbed as she stretched to dust the cubbies.

"There was a argue. My father hit our mother. He tole her he was gonna kill her. She say, 'Don't ever say that no more'!"

I gave up on preparing folders and went to Sharon. "That was frightening for you."

"Real scary," she nodded. "I was shakin'. He was drunk, and the argue last a long time. Our momma was cryin'."

"You must be angry at your father, Sharon."

She didn't look up but answered sadly, "We don't know where did he went. We still love him, but we wish we didn't knowed him."

"Eddie can't ride the bus no more!" was the first greeting from one of my pupils, minutes after Sharon left.

Behind Julie, Mr. Sargent, who had replaced our original driver, marched angrily toward me. The powerfully built man had Eddie tucked tightly under his arm, like a slippery football.

"No job's worth puttin' up with this." He dumped the boy at my feet. "First he makes trouble and won't sit where I can watch him. Next he opens the door while I'm drivin'. Coulda lost a kid. I'm through with him, ya hear?"

"I hate your crummy bus!" Eddie yelled from the floor. "You too. You're so wicked mean."

"Tell his mother," the driver called over his shoulder, en route to his van, "I ain't pickin' him up."

Eddie stood, hands cupped around his mouth to maximize the retort. "Tell my mother. So what? I won't hafta come!"

"Okay, Eddie." I put my arm around him. "What happened?"

"That driver's a bum." He twisted away from my touch. "If you talk about it, I'll scream. I'll run up and down the hall and throw everything around. I'll pollute the whole damn school."

"I see you're pretty angry." I walked into the room expecting him to follow. He remained in the hall.

Not one looked refreshed by vacation. Mechanically, Julie, Kevin, Douglas, and Jonathan put away coats and lunches and sat staring as if we were strangers.

"Good morning, Douglas." I patted his shoulder in passing.

"Shut up."

"Eddie's not the only unhappy one," I said. "Is it because of the bus ride?"

Silence.

"Maybe we should work a while and talk later."

I had learned that work, far more than play, helped these children pull themselves together.

Eddie finally appeared but clung to the wall, his hands and cheek pressed against it. In this strange position, as if by touch exploring the contours of the room, he gradually moved around to the reading table where I sat with Kevin.

I leaned back, to prevent him from passing. "I'd like you to sit with us."

"Get outta my way, dummy!" He pushed against me.

"See?" Douglas suddenly exploded, pointing at Eddie. "That's what I mean! Other kids know that punk's in my class! It's embarrassing. They think I'm crazy too!"

"That's corny, Douglas." Julie faced him scornfully, her hands on her hips. "You're crazy or you're not. It doesn't depend on Eddie."

Douglas looked momentarily confused, then apparently accepted Julie's philosophy. He continued his crossword puzzle.

Eventually, Eddie took his folder from my desk. "I'm not workin' near these nuts." He went into the "office." I sat beside him to help him start.

"I'll drive you home tonight, Eddie. Then we can talk about the transportation problem." He said nothing but paused in writing, and I was certain he'd listened.

Eleven o'clock. "Douglas' turn to read," I said. He usually came eagerly.

"Listen, stupid," was today's response. "Stop interfering with me! Can't you see I'm busy?"

"Me too, Doug. And it's our turn to read or neither of us will finish by noon."

He relented and headed slowly toward the reading table.

Kevin waited until Douglas was close enough, then clutched the leg of his gray corduroy pants. "Hey, why don't ya paint instead? Or play with blocks?"

"I'll get it over with, thanks," said the condemned reader. He flopped his bulky form onto the small chair near mine.

"Calling all cars." Holding his ruler like a microscope, Kevin spoke in a muffled voice. "Calling all cars. There's a crazy kid in this room. Come and get him. Over."

"Button up your lip!" Douglas yelled. Startled, Kevin dropped the prop.

"Maybe you don't get mad yourself," Douglas said to Kevin, "but you sure make other people mad."

The room settled into uneasy silence. Kevin, perhaps in deference to Douglas, removed his shoes and tapped in stocking feet. Her folder finished, Julie fed the doll a bottle, allowing herself an occasional taste. Soon it was equal time for each, until she abandoned the doll entirely and sucked without distraction.

In the "office," Eddie worked fitfully. "Think I can do this?" he said angrily.

"I'm sure you can," I replied.

Jonathan, also finished, now began to cut, tape, and fasten huge sheets of white construction paper into a mysterious form.

Douglas became captivated by the controlled reader, which flashed words and phrases at set intervals. In two months, his reading speed had doubled. When he reached across to adjust the machine's focus, I was startled to see that his arms were covered with a prickly rash.

"What's wrong?" I asked. Too fine for chicken pox. Maybe measles or roseola.

"Huh?" he examined himself, pulling up his white T-shirt to expose a spotted stomach.

"Has your brother had a rash, Doug? Or any kids you know?"

Douglas studied his body in alarm. "Luke's a mutation. They don't get rashes. What is it anyhow?"

"Nothing serious, I'm sure. Mrs. Rogers will know."

The nurse led him out and was back in minutes for his belongings. "German measles." She hurried to the door. "Second case today. Five before vacation. Looks like an epidemic. He'll be out at least a week. I'll bring him home."

Douglas' measles prevented him from participating in our first class with Bob Gough, the new physical education teacher. That afternoon he took the children to the gym. I poured coffee in the teachers' lounge, feeling both as relieved and anxious as a mother the first day of kindergarten.

Ten minutes into the scheduled hour, the young gym teacher returned my group. He appeared at the door of the lounge, rolled his eyes, and with a jerk of his head beckoned me to follow.

The children were lined up in the hall.

"Home at last," sighed Jonathan.

Bob blew his whistle sharply. "Right to your seats!"

They obeyed.

"I'm sorry, Mrs. Craig. Maybe we'll try again. They weren't ready today. Eddie, here, can't wait for directions. Kept knocking the ball from my arm." Eddie stuck out his tongue. "Kevin wouldn't let Julie have a chance. Said she couldn't catch." Kevin smiled. "This one," he pointed to Jonathan, "just flapped his arms and ran around the gym. I don't give flying lessons."

As Bob left, Eddie protested. "Selfish bum. Wouldn't let anyone else use the ball." But Eddie was calm, his words unconvincing. He was glad to be back.

Jonathan immediately began taping the paper sculpture he had worked on in the morning to a chair beside his own. "Oooeee. Squish, squish. You can stay if you don't wet your pants." Thus began a steady dialogue with the unresponsive occupant of that chair, a life-sized paper ghost.

Shortly before two, Eddie became more edgy. He'd watch the clock, then stretch to see out the window. The bus hadn't come.

When it did, and the others started to leave, he was ready to cry. I was supposed to send an inventory list to the office, but decided to do it later, rather than keep him waiting.

"Time for us to go too," I said.

He darted into the closet, crouched in a corner, and pulled his sweater over his head.

"You don't want me to drive you?"

He tumbled over, lying on his side, but, unlike other times, he spoke. "Whew! I thought you were trickin' me to get me on the bus."

I was surprised. "Have I ever tricked you?"

"Let's go! Let's go!" He quickly put on his sweater and handed me my jacket.

In the car, Eddie abruptly became distant, formal. Our relationship hadn't been tested beyond the classroom. He sat far to the right, leaving as much space between us as possible.

"I'm really hungry," I said. "Would you like a treat?"

"If you want to. Anyway I just had a little lunch. My mother forgot to go to the store."

We had hamburgers and cokes at a picnic table outside a drive-in restaurant. The sun was shining—not quite spring but full of promise. He ate but was unresponsive to my conversational overtures. Nor was he more talkative on the way home.

"I'll call your mother tonight. For a while she'll have to arrange to transport you, but maybe the bus driver will give you another chance. If he does, should I tell him you'll sit still and not make any more trouble?"

He nodded yes.

"Here," he said in front of an old wooden three-family house with sagging porches on each level. His hand was on the door handle before I stopped the car.

"Eddie," I wanted to leave him more relaxed, "at least the bus problem gave us a chance for a treat."

"I know one thing." He was outside, speaking through the half-opened window, "I had a good time, Mom."

He ran to the house.

# CHAPTER 26

Eddie's mother was furious when I phoned to tell her he wouldn't be transported. "I pay my taxes. They can't kick him off the bus."

"If his riding endangers himself and the others, I'm afraid they can," I said. "The most we can hope for is a short-term exclusion rather than a permanent one."

"I'm sick of everyone pickin' on my kid. He won't be there till this thing's settled. I'll call the superintendent if I have to." She hung up.

But Eddie did come the next day, breathless and twenty minutes early. I assumed his mother had relented.

"Am I late?" he panted. "Where are the kids? I ran all the way."

He had come three miles rather than miss school. Yet all that day he railed against being there.

Miss Silverstein had announced a teachers' meeting for after school. Knowing I couldn't drive Eddie, I had the secretary watch the class at noon while I called Mr. Brenner.

"I'm very willing to be involved," he said. "I'll pick him up at two. In fact I want to handle this with the mother and the bus driver. I think I'll propose a written contract between them, that both parties will be obliged to honor."

"What's this about a contract?" Eddie's mother screamed over the phone when she reached me at home that night. "I'm gonna see that man tomorrow, just to tell him he's crazy."

I heard nothing more about their meeting, but Mr. Brenner drove Eddie the rest of that week.

"I can't believe it!" Ceil said after a reasonably calm Friday. "Mr. Brenner is seeing Eddie's mother every day! Says he knows just how to handle her. He stops in, morning and afternoon, when he drives Eddie. She's through with the modeling course, so she's home now."

"Oh boy!" I said. "Can't wait to read that contract."

"He keeps telling me," she began to laugh, "that—that she won't take her eyes off him! What'll they do when Eddie is allowed back on the bus? That looks promising. The whole thing's not really funny," she giggled, wiping her eyes, "but I'd rather laugh than cry."

Monday morning, exactly a week after Douglas had been sent home with measles, a star-studded envelope was lying in my mailbox at school. Miss Silverstein, amused by the artwork, stood by as I opened it. I read the note and handed it to her.

It was strange without Douglas, yet his absence had its advantages. Kevin was less provocative, which made Julie happier. I had more opportunity to handle Eddie's behavior verbally, since upsets didn't develop into confrontations with Douglas. And there was extra time to spend with Jonathan.

Douglas' note and his continued absence occasioned a long recital of past illnesses and accidents involving his classmates.

"Once, slidin' down the hill on my sled, I crashed into a car," Julie said. "Got a percussion or something like that." She clutched her head.

"Baby ghost wet his pants down cellar. The mother wouldn't let him up, and he fell down the stairs. Oooo. Didn't you, bad boy?" Jonathan jiggled his desk mate.

Kevin looked wistful. "When I was a baby, I was always in the hospital. My mother tole me."

toDo

toDay AND
EVERY Day
I Miss
the Shcool
I Miss You
AND Eddie AND
Kevin. Love

(douglas)

"Don't think that's bad." Eddie paced fretfully, his hands in his pockets. "I fell outta the car. The door was broken. My mother stopped, but I coulda been kilt."

"Think any kids are in the hospital right now?" Julie asked.

"Course, dummy. There always are," Eddie said, still walking.

There followed a discussion of cousins, friends and even enemies who had at some time been hospitalized. After the kids left for the bus, Julie came back. She often returned for a good-bye hug or to share a last confidence. Today it was both.

"Since we sent stuff to Douglas, could we get some things for other kids who are sick? Kids in the hospital?"

"Why, that's a lovely idea! Let's talk about it tomorrow."

Driving home, I kept thinking of Julie's suggestion. Somehow it helped crystallize vague thoughts I'd had about the program. Total individualization had served its purpose. It was time now for group action and interplay, time for the children to become full-fledged members of the school and perhaps of the community. I would move from one-to-one instruction and ask Miss Silverstein to include our class in the cafeteria with the rest of the school. And what better way to gain self-respect than feeling we had something to share with others less fortunate? Julie's idea was more appropriate than she could realize.

With Kevin carrying his books, and Julie heralding his arrival, Douglas returned Tuesday morning, delivering an enthusiastic speech on keeping-busy-with-a-contagious-disease. "And I learned to cook corn pones and grits. See, down South, my grandmother useta cook for fancy people and. . . ."

When Julie finally got the opportunity, she repeated her idea of sending gifts to hospitalized children. Douglas became self-appointed chairman of the project. "I was sick last, so I know how it feels. Not that I didn't like the puzzle you sent or nothin', but if we give money, kids can get stuff they want. Money's better."

No one had money. The chairman allowed as how the jewels he once stashed behind the five-and-ten were probably rusted by now.

The night before, Ellie had been in the kitchen until after ten decorating brownies with blue and white peace symbols for a class sale. Now, with silent acknowledgment to her I proposed a bake sale for our class.

"Cool. Me and my grandmother'll make raisin cookies."

From that day on, my wish for group activities was realized. Even Jonathan worked on the posters that were proudly distributed to every class. Excitement mounted. Central School had never had a bake sale. Other children came to our room to ask about it.

Arithmetic time was devoted to making price signs. Debates were held on which class should come in first. Douglas, of course, opted for the oldest. Julie argued. "The little kids won't buy as much. Let them choose before everything's gone." Surprisingly, she won unanimously. Even Douglas was swayed.

I sent notes home, explaining the purpose of our sale and thanking parents in advance for their cooperation.

When the great day came, Julie dragged in a carton containing a hundred cellophane bags of popcorn. Kevin's mother drove him and delivered a chocolate sheet cake, cut into fifty servings. Mr. Brenner took Eddie to the store en route to school. He purchased twenty double packages of cream-filled cupcakes, each of which he sliced in quarters. Douglas ceremoniously removed the covers from the two shoe boxes he'd carried. Both were filled to the brim with plump golden raisin cookies.

Jonathan came empty-handed.

"You're the only one who forgot," Julie scolded.

"You bum!" Eddie said.

Jonathan sought solace with his paper friend, but both were relegated to a corner in preparation for the customers. The merchants stood behind double desks, on which they spread the goods. There was a hectic scramble to sort out price tags, and a frantic search for the magic marker when Douglas insisted that none of the prepared cards indicated the true worth of his cookies.

"Ten cents each," he insisted.

"For one cookie?" said Eddie. "You're flaky."

"I'm chargin' five cents for my cake," said Kevin.

"Five cents is fair for everything," Julie decreed.

"Now listen," Douglas thrust a cookie in her face, "these have eggs and margarine and genuine raisins. Do you know how long it takes one single grape to become a raisin?"

"They're beautiful," I said, "but if you charge too much, kids won't be able to afford them."

"Okay, okay, five cents." He held up his hands in resignation. "But for five cents they're not getting raisins."

At nine-fifteen the first graders filed into our room. At the same time, Jonathan's mother appeared and left a tray of candied apples. Julie quickly arranged a desk for Jonathan, who with his paper ghost was recalled from the corner. He and his silent partner sold every apple.

Douglas did not participate. He'd moved his wares to the "office," where he stood with his back to the class.

By the time the second graders arrived, he, too, was in business —a mound of crumbling de-raisined cookies on one desk, tiny piles of raisins on the other, both products labeled "5c Each."

The last group of sixth graders left at eleven-thirty. By now the room was a shambles, desks and floor littered with waxed paper, crumbs, candy-apple sticks, and mashed popcorn. But from the beginning the event was a social success. Children who were reluctant to enter our room, having heard who-knows-what about its occupants, found it not only safe but perhaps even enviable.

"Hey, you got only five kids and all this audiovisual jazz?" one sixth grader said admiringly.

"You're lucky, getting to have a cake sale," a little girl told Julie.

I was delighted with the effect of such recognition, particularly on Kevin and Jonathan. As the morning progressed they changed from mumbling self-effacing boys to confident salesmen, enjoying positions of authority.

Miss Silverstein was our last customer. She bought everyone's leftovers and lingered to hear Douglas announce the final tally. Eleven dollars and thirty cents, all but one dollar in small change.

"Boss!" Douglas said. "That's a lotta bread!"

"Will you bring it to the hospital today," Julie asked me, "and tell 'em it's from us?"

"Better yet," Miss Silverstein paused in the doorway, "I'll call now and let their office know how hard you worked."

Although we now had permission to eat in the cafeteria, the children asked to remain in our room. Over lunch, they relived details of the exciting morning.

"Did ya see the boy who bought five cakes and just ate the frosting?"

"And the little kid with a whole dollar?"

"I brought extra popcorn." Julie distributed a bag to each. Douglas rejected his. "I'm not hungry." He hadn't touched his lunch.

"I know why." Kevin turned to Douglas. "I saw ya stuffing your face with raisins."

"So what? I'm a raisin freak!"

Everyone laughed.

Each child voluntarily shared in cleaning the room. The only fight concerned who would be first with the broom. Douglas finally surrendered it to Eddie. "But now he owes me a spectacular favor."

The intercom buzzed. It was Miss Silverstein. "I have Mr. Mollo, public relations director at the hospital, on the line. I need your opinion. He's inviting you and the children to bring the money in person, and he'll provide a tour of the hospital. What do you think?"

"That's great. Any day next week would be fine. I'll tell the children."

# CHAPTER 27

The happiness engendered by Tuesday's bake sale and the invitation to the hospital remained with us all Wednesday and Thursday. Friday, I was sure, would round out our first perfect week.

I had planned a day without pressure. Since this Sunday, May eighth, would be Mother's Day, each child could choose from a variety of projects or work on several.

With every class I had previously taught, I set aside a day before each holiday just for making presents. These were days the children especially enjoyed, and I decided to try it now with my Transitional Class.

Before school, Paul, Sharon and two new visitors helped me arrange a corner for making paper flowers, a paint and clay area, a weaving table with potholder materials, and the workbench with a variety of tools.

They left when the bell rang, giving me a few minutes to reflect on the one part of the day I dreaded. Ceil and I had scheduled an after school conference with Eddie's mother, to approach the subject of residential treatment. Without her cooperation we could proceed no further. I wondered how she would react.

Eddie's voice interrupted my thoughts. "Why'd you change the room?" With both hands he swept the weaving material onto the floor. "You know I hate things moved!"

Holding his wrists, I knelt to look directly in his eyes. "That was okay earlier, Ed, when we didn't know each other as well. Not anymore. Look at you. Today you have on a brown shirt. Yesterday you wore a sweater." He looked down at his clothes. "I know you're still you, even though you look different. Why does it matter if furniture is rearranged? You know this is your room. Those things aren't important when people trust each other."

"Goddamnit! They matter to me! Some man was having coffee in my chair this morning when I wanted to have breakfast. I can't stand people who take my things!"

"Eddie, stop being so mean." Julie tucked a yo-yo in her cubby. "Mrs. Craig worked hard to put that stuff out." She looked around. "What's it for, anyway?"

"For you to make Mother's Day presents." I released Eddie's wrists. He sank to the floor and lay motionless.

Douglas stepped over Eddie's body to confront me at close range. "Mother's Day, huh? Then I don't have to do anything. Might as well go home." He turned as if he were leaving but paused after a few steps.

"I thought you'd like to make something for your grandmother," I said.

I had spoken to Doug, but Kevin answered.

"Yeah." He looked out the window. "I don't know why, but every time my grandmother comes, I feel happier. Why don't ya make a present for your grandmother, Doug?"

Douglas clutched the lapel of Kevin's red jacket. "Listen pal, just 'cause you got a mother, no wisecracks from you."

Kevin's eyes grew wide as he stared at Douglas' restraining hand.

"That wasn't a wisecrack," Julie said, stirring a jar of red paint. "You're just feeling sorry for yourself, Douglas."

Embarrassed, Douglas slid his hand up Kevin's lapel to pat him on the shoulder. "Listen ole buddy. I just grabbed ya cause I'm not used to you makin' speeches. You shook me up." He laughed self-consciously. "You used to talk with your feet, remember?"

Kevin looked at his shoes. "My mother doesn't like me to talk."

Douglas cocked his head quizzically. "You mean she'd rather have you tap?"

"Uh-uh." Kevin didn't look up. "She'd rather have me nothin'."

Eddie chose some boards from the wood carton and went right to the workbench. Douglas sat cross-legged on the floor, threading the loom. Jonathan, also on the floor, sat by the bucket of clay, toying absently with a handful. Gradually he worked the clay more intensely. He rocked back and forth, making sounds, "mmmm, mmmm," as the softened material began to ooze through his fingers.

Kevin could not be coaxed from his chair, but Julie was ready to paint. She asked me to button her "art shirt," an old one of her father's, so long on her that the tail flapped against the Band-Aid on her knee.

She clipped a large paper to the easel and painted a radiant sun in the upper right-hand corner. "This is gonna be where I used to live. I think it was Idaho. No, it was Ohio. I went to a park there once, with my other mother."

Jonathan, eyes closed with a blissful expression, smeared the clay up both arms and onto his neck. "Mmm. Gushy, gushy." He rubbed it on his cheeks. "Gushy, mmmm."

Julie painted grass and a row of yellow and red tulips. Suddenly, slashing with the paint brush, she spread a huge brown X over the idyllic scene.

"Oh, I don't know who I went to the park with. I always dis-remember!" She tore the paper from the clips. "I'm throwin' this away. Nothin' I make is any good."

"Me neither." Eddie kept hammering. "Anyway my mother don't like dumb presents kids make." His voice was rising. "And I know something else she doesn't like. A two-letter word—M-E." His head lowered, Eddie concentrated fiercely on the project, which was beginning to look suspiciously like a machine gun. "If this doesn't work, I'm gonna get mad!"

"Blow your top if you want to," Douglas grimaced, rubbing his shoulder. "Just don't do any biting."

Kevin sat at his desk, staring vacantly. "I think my mother likes me sometimes." He spoke as if he'd been silently debating the issue. "She lets me sleep in her bed when they have a fight. In the morning I like to put my hands in her bureau and mess up all her stuff."

"I'd never do that," said Julie. Calmer now, she began another painting. "I just like to touch my mother's stuff and smell the perfume. But it makes my father mad cause it costs so much."

"Yeah, I know about them women," Douglas quickly assumed

a fencing position, ruler outthrust, "who run all over the place yelling 'Charge'!"

Julie giggled. "Oh, Douglas you're funny." She had been painting all morning, but the only evidence was her work shirt, stained with blotches of every color. Each picture, still wet, had landed in the wastebasket.

Several times, I had moved toward Kevin, hoping to get him started, but he slipped away to sit pensively in another corner of the room. By lunchtime only Douglas' potholder was close to completion.

For the past two days our class had joined others in the lunchroom, but today it didn't seem feasible. It would have taken the entire period to wash Julie and unmold Jonathan. Cubby doors slammed as paper bags and metal lunchboxes were removed.

"Ugh!" Kevin spat a mouthful of sandwich onto his desk. "She knows I hate salami!" He dumped the contents of his lunchbox into the wastebasket.

"You shoulda seen what we had last night," Julie said. "My mother made me eat it all. I almost threw up. When I have children I'll never make them eat stuff they hate."

"I never get anything I like." Kevin slid his empty lunchbox into his cubby. While his back was turned, Douglas, having gobbled up his own, retrieved Kevin's food from the wastebasket.

Eddie arranged his lunch on the workbench and bit into an apple. "I know one thing," he chewed as he talked. "If your parents aren't good to you, kids should be allowed to choose new ones."

"That's a good idea. I think my mother hates—" Julie stopped. She bit her lower lip. "—little kids."

"I know how ya tell." Kevin sat picking at his fingernails. "If your mother doesn't yell, it means she doesn't care."

Douglas sank his teeth in the second half of Kevin's sandwich. "Does your mother yell?" He looked up.

"Uh-uh." Kevin began to tap.

Douglas rolled the waxed paper into a mini-basketball and took several shots at the wastebasket.

"Everybody done?" I asked. "We don't have much time. Let's get back to work on our presents."

“My grandmother really needs this.” Douglas picked up the loom. Just a few more rows and the potholder would be finished.

“Your grandmother, your grandmother!” Eddie mimicked. “Where’s your mother, anyway?”

Uncertain just how provocative Eddie had meant to be, Douglas half rose, fists clenched, but made no further move. “She hadda go away. She couldn’t help it.”

“Did she die?”

He sank into his chair, his head cradled in his hands. “No, she just went away. I think she had tired blood.”

No longer interested, Eddie admired his gun, sighting over the barrel as he cocked his finger on the trigger.

Julie took her paper off the easel and laid it on the floor. She had painted two heads. The larger one had four eyes, the smaller had none. She dipped her hand into the jar of red paint, then knelt by the picture and smeared both faces until the weakened paper tore.

She didn’t stop when the paper ripped, but rotated her hands on the newspaper beneath until that too was red. “Pretend the mother kills the child,” she said softly, “and they’re both all covered with blood.”

I hesitated, not wanting to interrupt, but when it seemed she would say no more, I asked. “Why would the mother do that?”

“She hates the child. She hates her little girl.” Julie didn’t look at me. She stared intently at the papers. “She just got stuck with her.”

“She didn’t want her?”

“Course not. The girl’s real mean. She calls her mother bad words. But she feels better now. She’s dead and she’s happy.” From a kneeling position, Julie sat back on her heels, her hands motionless. “She doesn’t wanna get in any more trouble.”

“The girl didn’t like being in trouble.” I wasn’t sure she was listening.

“No. She’s not mad anymore,” Julie said quietly.

“I see.” I bent to speak directly to her. “Then she used to be mean because she was angry.”

“Mmm.” Julie looked at her hands as if she were amazed to find them red. “Take my shirt off! Quick! I’ve gotta go wash!”

I undid the buttons. “Don’t worry, Julie. It comes right off.”

Arms outstretched, she ran to the bathroom. I cleaned up the mess and sponged the floor around it.

"Kevin, why don't you paint for a while?" He sat stiffly, hands folded, and didn't answer.

"Don't you think your mother would like a picture?"

He looked at me, then got up slowly and went to the closet where his work shirt was kept. I was pleased that he would accept my suggestion, but stepping inside, he quietly pulled the door shut. A second later the lock clicked softly.

"You don't have to do that, Kevin." I didn't try to approach him. "It's all right to say you don't feel like painting."

The door opened a crack, enough for a polished black toe to poke through. Then, one behind the other, his loafers slid into the room.

Here we go again, I thought. "I'm glad at least your shoes are with us," I said aloud, "but I wish you'd join them."

A hand reached out near the bottom of the door and rocked the nearer shoe. Heel-toe. Heel-toe.

"Goddamnit! Everybody's always yelling!" Eddie hurled the hammer against the cork bulletin board.

"You're through there, Eddie." Trembling at the thought that someone might have been hurt, I picked up the hammer and put it in the drawer. "If you throw tools, you're not ready to use them."

"I hate people like you!" he screamed, grabbing the wooden gun. "Rat-a-tat-tat. Rat-a-tat-tat. I hate all you bastards."

Jonathan, now caked with clay, scurried to his desk. Cupping his hands around his mouth he bent to direct his words down the empty inkwell. "S-K-5. Calling S-K-5. They're penetrating our defenses. Check the radar."

"Who are you talking to, Jonathan?" Hoping to put a quick end to this aberration, I lifted his desktop. "I don't see anyone here."

"Whew! Good getaway, S-K-5!" He went back to the clay.

Eddie was still shooting. "Rat-a-tat-tat!" At first I was barely aware of the muffled sounds from Douglas, resting on his desk, his head buried in his arms.

"Doug, what's wrong?" He raised his head, revealing the concealed loom. Every thread hung loose, completely unraveled. With his elbow he shoved it off the desk. Giving one heave, he tossed his desk on its side, then leaped up, grabbing his chair by the rung. Holding it out, he began to spin.

Gun in hand, Eddie darted behind my desk. "Oh, no! Not again! Every man for himself! Take cover!"

"S-K-5!" Jonathan rushed to the inkwell. "Are you on duty?"

"Douglas!" I yelled. "Put that down before you get in trouble!"

He twirled faster and faster. "I hate her. I hate her. I hope she never comes back!"

Returning from washing, Julie heard Douglas' words at the doorway. "Oh, no! I didn't do nothin' to him!" She burst into tears as she ran to her seat.

Douglas began teetering. "Dizzy, dizzy." He let go of the chair. It shot across the room and banged against the front panel of my desk, leaving a deep gouge in the wood. He tried to brace himself against the wall. "Oooeee! The room's goin' round and round!" He sank to the floor, his back against the radiator. Breathing deeply, he sat motionless for a moment. Gradually his whole body began to tremble. He rolled back his head, eyes blindly riveted on the ceiling. At first he made guttural noises, like gargling, but suddenly he burst out with a high keening wail.

Jonathan clapped his hands over his ears. The closet door squeaked. Kevin retracted his loafers.

Douglas' shrieks rose and fell with terrifying intensity. His face contorted in tearless anguish. Then his words became audible. "Mother, why? why? Oh, Mother, why?" From leaning back, he fell forward, hunching like an animal. "Oh Mother, Mother. Why? Why? Oh, Mother, why?" He cried a long time, venting his unbearable grief in terrible choking sounds.

When much of his sorrow seemed spent, I went to him, searching for the right words. But it was impossible for me to speak. Hesitantly, I put my hand on his shoulder.

"She'll never come back," he moaned, "never."

"Douglas, Douglas, I'm sorry. You miss her so." I knelt to comfort him. He put his head on my lap and sobbed. Patting his back, I looked around the room at the visible consequences of this day, the wastebasket brimming with soggy paintings, the ruined potholder dangling from the loom, the overturned desk and damaged furniture.

Eddie, still cowering behind my desk, pressed the gun against his face. Julie, whining, sat wringing her skirt with both hands. Jonathan's pencil made a scratching sound as he tried to drill through his desktop. Kevin stared from the closet, his shoes clutched to his chest.

Time alone would measure the cost of this setback—weeks, perhaps months—the price of my insistence on a meaningless gesture of gift giving.

The tires squealed as the bus pulled in. Kevin, stocking-footed, moved automatically toward the hall. Julie, Jonathan, and Eddie followed silently. I helped Douglas up and walked him to the parking lot. No one turned to wave.

"I was asking them to demonstrate a love that was never there or is totally inexpressible, after you and I've worked months to help them express real emotions."

Ceil didn't sympathize. "Look, you've learned something valuable. In the process, believe me, they expressed real emotion. More than you were prepared to unleash. Stop beating your breast. If you want penance, here comes Eddie's mother."

Mrs. Conte looked younger than I'd remembered. Perhaps it was her clothes, a hot pink pants suit, or that her hair was down, curling girlishly about her face. She sat to my right. Skillfully, Ceil led the conference from generalities to a discussion of Eddie's behavior. My role was to summarize his activities in school, the problems, glimmers of progress, his tremendous anxiety and how it interfered with his learning.

Mrs. Conte sat back eyeing me without comment.

Ceil leaned toward her. "Do you see any relationship between the upsets he's had here and his behavior at home?"

Before answering, Mrs. Conte lit a cigarette. "Listen, I don't keep records. That kid's worse every day. Almost burned the house down. No other kids are allowed near him. Even my girl friend won't bring her son over. I'm supposed to pay for three windows he's broken. Every time I go out he does somethin'. Twice he's cut electric cords. Say he likes gettin' shocked. Last night I was tellin' him to watch out for his sister. He told me to get closer, like he wanted to kiss me good-bye. He pissed on my best dress." She stubbed out the cigarette angrily.

Ceil waited, but Mrs. Conte didn't continue.

"Eddie's having trouble at home and in school, even in special class. We have no place else to offer, Mrs. Conte," she said. "Putting him on homebound would be worse for both of you. We believe he needs more help than we can give."

"Maybe there's somethin' wrong with his brain," his mother said. "The kid's never been happy. I dunno why."

Ceil answered slowly, in a gentle voice. "Do you remember the mothers' group when I explained the difference between organic problems and those that are emotional? Eddie's brain is fine, organically. The kind of help I'm suggesting is a school with intensive treatment for emotional problems."

"You mean he should go away?" It was hard to judge her reaction.

"It's our recommendation," Ceil nodded. "That doesn't mean you have to accept it."

Don't! I wanted to yell. Say you want your son at home!

"I could've told you long ago that's what he needed." She sounded annoyed. "It's one terrible day after another wonderin' what that kid'll do next. I've gotta live too, ya know." She twisted a strand of black hair around her index finger. "Let someone else try with him. I've got other problems."

She bit her thumbnail pensively, then looked up and said. "The agency told me if I cut my hair I'll get a job right away. I dunno. My boy friend likes it long."

# CHAPTER 28

Sunday, May eighth, was Mother's Day. Voices rose in disagreement from the kitchen, followed by fierce whispering on the stairs. A breakfast tray was carried in by four tiptoeing servants who sat on the bed to watch me eat. On the tray, a rose, bacon omelette, blueberry muffins, and coffee so black it made Bill's eyes bulge.

I stayed in bed reading the paper while the children cleaned the kitchen. Actually, I was half reading, half listening to their running arguments over who was to wash the dishes and who to dry. Ann said the water was too cold, Billy said it was too hot. Ellie was squeezing in too much dishwashing liquid. But the discussion dissolved into giggling as I heard Billy exclaim, "Oh, Madam, surely you won't do all these dishes! Your hands are tooo lovely!"

At one o'clock, feeling sheepish, I started to dress and discovered a light rash on both arms. Within an hour my German measles were highly visible.

Miss Silverstein and I had occasionally talked of how to find suitable substitutes, but had never come to any conclusion. Invariably her final remark was, "Just don't get sick!" When I phoned, she sighed at the prospect of getting someone for a week.

"My planbook's in the middle drawer," I said, "and would you postpone our trip to the hospital?"

"Only if you'll get well quickly. How I'll miss you with that gang on my hands."

In spite of the fever and a very sore throat, it was nice being home with my family. "You're not to get up," Bill announced. "I'm in charge of the troops, and we're going to see some discipline around here." Ann rolled her eyes toward the ceiling.

Still, during the week I noticed that the kids responded to Bill's directions faster than they ever did to mine. I read and slept a lot, but from nine to two each day I couldn't help but wonder what was going on in my class.

Ceil stopped by Thursday afternoon. "Well today was the low point," she reported, "a Mrs. Hines substituted. Yesterday she promised to bring in her daughter's guinea pig, if everyone would be good. She did today, and Eddie broke its back. Said he just felt like squeezing it. Mrs. Hines was almost hysterical. She ran to the office with the dead animal in her hand. Miss Silverstein told Eddie's mother to keep him out the rest of the week."

"Poor guinea pig! Well, I'll be in Monday, I'm sure."

"Thank goodness. I've stopped by every day. The kids really miss you. Last Monday they had an awfully sweet woman, but you know how they mistake softness for weakness. The room was wild. She told me Kevin started it by throwing pencils at her! When I asked him about it, Douglas told me to leave him alone. Said he didn't blame Kevin. He felt like doing it too."

I laughed.

"You'll enjoy the letters they wrote." She put on her coat. "And Miss Silverstein will be delighted to know you're better." I read and reread their notes.

But I didn't go back Monday. Over the weekend my fingers had swollen, as fat and shapeless as German sausages, and terribly painful. The doctor didn't sound surprised.

"It's a particularly virulent strain of measles. Many adults, especially women, are having arthritic-like complications. You'll feel better if you apply heat. Take aspirin as often as you want, but the swelling will last several days."

Every joint ached. Aspirin didn't get close to the pain. Lying in bed, I tried not to dwell on being absent from my class. Friday, Miss Silverstein called with comforting news.

"Since Tuesday we've had a marvelous sub. An off-duty airline pilot, if you can imagine. He's had training and wants to teach when he retires. Douglas complained the first day. He came to tell me Mr. Knox was trying to butter him up. And Julie was afraid

Dear Mrs. Craig,
I love you.
And I like you too.
And I hope you get well.
And I hope you come back.
And I like you very much.

love,
Kevin

Dar Mrs. Craig
I get Well Soon please.

I hop you feel well
pleas get well

Did you have to get sick
get well for affee One
in the class

love

Douglas

ghost's wish

Boo
Hoo! booo
get Well

BaBy

Boo

Back

Wet
Pants

(from Jonathan)

Central school

Dear Mrs Graig

Hi Mrs craig. I hope you feel goD.
You will get well.
I hope you can come BaK to school
Come BaK to school soon.
By Mrs craig.

Eddie

Dear. Mrs. Craig I wish,
you can get well. If you get. my
wish I wish to you, I'm
giving you a surprise Love, Julie

of him, as you might expect. She hid in the nurse's office a few times, but things were much smoother than last week. Now how about you? Bill says it's been rough."

"Whatever happened to simple old measles? But the swelling's finally going. I'm coming next week, definitely."

"Good news! Oh, Eleanor, by the way, we received releases from Eddie's mother to forward his records to Green Valley. Kirby School is out. The town won't finance his going to a private facility when there's an opening in a state institution. I'm satisfied that Green Valley's the better place for him anyway, and I'm pleased things are moving so quickly."

"Oh," I paused, not wanting to reveal my disappointment at Eddie's leaving. Foolishly, I'd clung to the hope that the threat of his being sent away would bring about a dramatic change in his mother.

"I'll have the papers ready Monday," I said.

Since the day we visited the schools, I thought often of the harsh discipline I had witnessed at Green Valley, and the gentle less-demanding approach at Kirby. Which would be better for Eddie? I was angry that we had no more moderate choice, just these two extremes.

The Board of Education's decision that he go to a state institution settled the question now, but overall I felt as Ceil did, that this was also the more appropriate place. I remembered the young man we'd seen at Kirby who'd been there eighteen years. I didn't want that to happen to Eddie. Green Valley was geared toward returning children to the community. Expectations were higher. It seemed more hopeful.

On my first day back I was surprised that somehow the children looked older. Or was it that seeing them daily I had become immune to subtle evidence of growth? They seemed to think I was different too, because Monday was unique for its strained silence. Although we began group work that day, no one spoke other than to reply to a question.

Jonathan clutched his ghost close to him throughout the day. After lunch we watched a film. The screen didn't get snapped, nor the lights flicked. No one wiggled a hand in the projector's beam. Julie delivered the film to the office, Douglas packed the machine, Kevin raised the curtains. Then they just waited, hands folded.

I sat on the corner of my desk. "Thank you for the notes. I really enjoyed them."

Silence. There was a definite feeling of distance.

"You certainly kept the room neat. I appreciate that too."

Kevin squirmed. Julie's lower lip trembled. Douglas yawned and looked at the clock.

"I missed you all."

"Sure you did." Douglas spat the words sarcastically.

"What's that supposed to mean?"

"Listen, lady. I've had measles, remember? It doesn't take two weeks to get better."

"Oh, Doug!" I might have laughed if he hadn't looked so vulnerable. "You're right. The measles lasted a week. Then I had a complication, something like arthritis. Look." What a strange situation—to be grateful certain fingers were still swollen!

"Hmmm." He gently supported my palm for a closer inspection.

"Oh dear," Julie said. "They look sore."

"Are you gonna be sick again?" Eddie leaped up. "Cause if you are, don't get that bitch who kicked me out!"

"Yeah. She kept hollerin' at us to shut up, but she gave us candy all the time," Kevin said. "I dunno why."

"The reason she gave us candy," Douglas dropped my hand and turned to Kevin, "is she was doin' somethin' wrong all the time, and she didn't want to lose her job."

Jonathan jiggled self-consciously. "You forgot t' tell those people I'm a ghost. They didn't believe me."

"I'll bet that's because you're such a good-looking boy." I smiled.

He flushed and crossed his eyes. "I told you! I only pretend to be a boy."

The last ten minutes were no longer quiet. Yet at two o'clock, each child checked the Leaders Chart, then took his place in line, with none of the usual squabbling.

After class, I filled out Eddie's record and addressed the envelope to Green Valley. Reluctantly, I mailed it on the way home.

# CHAPTER 29

On Wednesday of that week we finally went to the hospital to donate our bake sale money. All but Eddie came dressed up. He seemed more neglected than ever, in a frayed flannel shirt that lacked two middle buttons. His face and hands were grimy, his hair disheveled. He reminded me of a war orphan.

Kevin looked handsome, his blond hair slickly groomed, his soft brown eyes enhanced by the camel color of his jacket. Douglas wore a white shirt, so well starched it crackled when his arms moved. Although Jonathan toyed uncomfortably with the lapel of his navy-blue suit, it made him look older and slimmer. And Julie, in her "goodest pink dress" with matching ribbons on her pigtails, was so pleased with herself that she pirouetted down the hall.

Miss Silverstein had offered to accompany us, but I wanted to take them alone and agreed to return if we had any problems. As a deterrent, we had a discussion of rules.

Eddie contributed number one. "Doors closed till the car stops." The second was Julie's idea. "No calling bad names like bastard." Douglas supplied the clincher. "No fighting, no biting, no Irish dynamiting!"

One final question had to be settled before we could leave. An argument was brewing as to who should present the money. Douglas cited his credentials, both as oldest and most recently sick. Eddie screamed that being a better reader entitled him to make the speech.

"Let's decide with anagrams." I held the box while each child chose. Kevin won with letter C, but his victory upset him. Pale and shaken, he thrust the envelope of money at Douglas as we headed for my car. "You give it to them. I don't wanna."

"Thanks, pal," Douglas grabbed it.

Julie donned her rhinestone sunglasses to make the trip, which took just ten minutes. We parked in the shadow of the huge brick building, and the children clustered around me anxiously on the walk to the entrance.

Jonathan refused to follow Julie through the self-opening doors. Beads of perspiration shimmering on his forehead, he clung to the wrought-iron railing outside.

"What made them open?" He stared at the doors. "Ghosts? Magic?"

"Don't be afraid. They work by motor. You'll be able to hear it." I pulled him through the doors to the waiting room.

The gaudily painted receptionist peered over the counter. "Wait here, please. Mr. Mollo will be right along."

We could hear his light footsteps before he was visible. A small, dapper man, he shook hands with me and each child in turn. "Ah, welcome," he smiled.

Douglas offered the envelope. "The kids and me—" But Mr. Mollo shook his head. "Not yet son. Come to my office."

We trailed him through the bustling corridor to a small room where a photographer waited. "You see," Mr. Mollo spoke warmly, "your idea is so thoughtful and the money so badly needed that we're going to put your picture in the paper."

The children posed stiffly except for Jonathan, who burped and crossed his eyes. After five or six flashes, the photographer nodded and left.

"Before we begin," Mr. Mollo said, "you should know you won't see any children. No patients at all."

"Damn it," Eddie snapped his fingers.

"Sorry, it's a hospital rule. But I can show you how the place runs. You can see the kitchens, the laundry, and the laboratories we have to help us get people well."

I was concerned that the tour might be depersonalized, but the children followed him eagerly. They marveled at the huge pans in the enormous kitchen. We cut through a storage room to the noisy, steamy laundry where Mr. Mollo shouted statistics above the clatter: ". . . and one thousand sheets every day, plus six hundred gowns and all the baby bedding. . . ."

The confusion was upsetting to Eddie, who looked ready to

bolt. Although he relaxed a little when I moved closer, it was a relief to leave the laundry. We went by elevator to the basement laboratories.

"We can't go in," Mr. Mollo said, "but you may look through the window. These people tell the doctors what they learn from their microscopes about a patient's disease."

A woman in a physician's smock stepped off the elevator and wheeled her mobile equipment table toward us.

Mr. Mollo motioned in her direction. "Here comes a special kind of doctor. She takes blood samples."

"Ugh." Julie shivered.

"It's nice to see young visitors," she said as she approached.

"My doctor wears one of them." Eddie pointed to her stethoscope.

"Would you like to try it? Leave it on my tray when you finish." She picked up a carton of test tubes and entered the lab.

I adjusted the stethoscope on Eddie. "Bar-ump, bar-ump! That's what my heart's doin'!" he shouted gleefully.

After everyone had a turn, Mr. Mollo led the way through swinging doors, marked "X-ray." All the children followed except Jonathan, who lingered by the tray and hestitantly tried the stethoscope again. His enraptured expression persuaded me to wait.

With his right hand he cupped the stethoscope to his chest. His left hand marked the rhythm he heard, as if he were conducting an orchestra. He undid his belt, lowered the instrument to his stomach and listened intently. Back to his chest, then to his stomach again, and finally, he held it over his penis. He stood motionless for a moment, shook his head negatively, and raised the stethoscope once more to his heart. At last he placed the instrument back on the tray.

"What did it sound like" I asked.

Jonathan, buckling his belt, replied, "I heard it beat! I heard it beat!" His voice filled with wonder, he kept repeating the words as I led him in pursuit of the group.

We found them peering into a tiny room at a monstrous silver machine being described as "one hundred thousand dollars worth of equipment."

Mr. Mollo turned to glance at Jonathan, then at me, his eyebrows raised questioningly. I nodded that all was well. No one else seemed aware of our absence.

"Well, I hope you learned something about hospitals today," he smiled, ringing for the elevator. "Are there any questions?"

"Oh, look!" Julie pointed down the hall.

A masked nurse, an infant in her arms, was leaving one of the X-ray rooms. She stood some distance away, but her eyes crinkled above the gauze, and she raised her elbow to make the child more visible. The dark-skinned baby was deeply asleep. His lips twitched in a sucking motion.

"You can't tell if that kid's black or white," Douglas mused.

"Red," Eddie said.

Julie was concerned. "Is he sick?"

"The doctor just wanted his foot X-rayed. Nothing serious." The nurse adjusted the receiving blanket. "See? He's fine. He slept through the whole thing."

"It's a black kid, all right," Douglas nodded. "They're much braver."

"Ha!" Eddie's hands were on his hips. "How come you squawked like a chicken when I bitcha?"

Fortunately, the elevator arrived. We thanked Mr. Mollo and shook hands again in the waiting room. I whisked Jonathan through the "magic door" before he thought to resist. All the way back to school, babies were the topic of discussion.

"I wonder what his heart sounds like," Jonathan said softly.

"I bet the mother's worried about his foot." Julie fiddled with her hair.

"Fathers worry too, smarty-farty." Kevin kept looking out the window.

"Or else he doesn't have one." Douglas flipped through a magazine he'd found on the back seat.

"What a dummy! Who d'ya think planted the seed?" Eddie challenged angrily.

"So?" Julie, beside me on the front seat, turned sideways to face Eddie. "That doesn't mean he'll really have a father. Besides, just because he grew in his mother's tummy, she still might not keep him. What if he's bad?"

I wouldn't have chosen the stop at a traffic light as the location at which to deal with anything so important. But neither could I let the moment pass.

"Being bad would have nothing to do with such a decision, Julie." I spoke slowly. "A mother who gives her baby up does it because she's not able to take care of him. She wants what's best for the baby because she loves him so much. That's the reason she would plan for her child to go to new parents who would also love him very much. Do you understand?"

Julie began sucking the tip of her pigtail. She nodded yes and cuddled close to me, wrapping both arms around my right sleeve. It was difficult to turn into the parking lot without jarring her. I switched off the motor, but no one stirred.

"You should be very proud of yourselves," I said. "First you raised money for the hospital, and then you behaved so well there today." Julie sat up. Kevin's smile was reflected in the rear-view mirror.

I started to get out, but Douglas dashed around the car to open my door. When I thanked him, he bowed deeply. "Anything for a lady."

I didn't notice the magazine still in his hand until he cupped it to his mouth like a megaphone: "Miss Silverstein!" he yelled, as we reached the first step. "Miss Silverstein! We saw a new baby!"

The next morning, for the first time, Jonathan came in ahead of his classmates and hurried to my desk. I thought he wanted to show me something, but he just leaned toward me, breathlessly. I had never seen him so bright-eyed.

"You're pretty excited about something."

He nodded and began hopping from one foot to the other in a kind of jig.

"Doesn't it feel funny?" he asked.

I was really puzzled. "What feels funny, Jonathan?"

"Doesn't it feel funny to wake up in the morning and say 'who am I'?" He took several skipping steps toward his cubby, then stopped to wrap his arms around his body in an intense self-embrace. His voice shaking, he spoke again, this time more to himself than to me. "Doesn't it feel funny to wake up in the morning and be a human being?"

All day I watched him with pleasure. He would suddenly stop working to scrutinize each fingernail or the creases in his palm.

When it was time to leave, Jonathan ceremoniously snipped the Scotch tape that bound his paper friend to the chair. I thought he'd take it home, but on the way out he stuffed his ghost into the wastebasket, stamped on it once, and briskly walked away, his head held high.

# CHAPTER 30

> To all members: The Transitional Class Planning Committee will convene in the Administration Building at 2:30 on Friday.

The memo was signed "J. Brenner."

I drove over, fuming that this meeting had been delayed so long. It was postponed once because of my illness, but even that original date was too late for the kind of planning I'd envisioned. Now, on May twenty-seventh, with school almost over, how could we possibly effect a gradual transition for any child?

Mr. Brenner became my scapegoat. He should have been more efficient. I dreaded having to see him that afternoon. But he wasn't with the other committee members at the long oak table. Nor was Ceil, who arrived fifteen minutes late.

"Sorry to keep you waiting." Her face was tense. "We've been trying to locate Mr. Brenner, who's supposed to chair this meeting. I've no idea where he is, so it's up to you what you want to do."

"Since he's in charge of the program," one of the social workers said, "it doesn't make sense to go ahead without him. We really couldn't make any decisions."

"That's true," someone agreed.

Whether it was my antipathy to Mr. Brenner or the threat of having the meeting canceled, I found myself seething with a kind of anger I rarely experienced. I felt hot and flushed, almost dizzy.

I jumped up. "But this is the most important meeting we'll have!" I felt everyone's eyes studying me. "We're finally at the point of discussing who's made progress and the best plan for each kid next year. As it is, we're two weeks late because I was sick.

Let's not postpone it again! There's as least one child who ought to be tried in regular class. If we delay, we'll never provide the kind of step-by-step transition we've spent so long planning. The year's almost over."

Suddenly I felt foolish. I should have calmed down, not spoken so emotionally. "No wonder she likes teaching those kids," I imagined them thinking. I sat down, not looking at anyone.

I heard some papers being shuffled, and one of the men cleared his throat. Then Miss Silverstein spoke. "I'd like to proceed with the original agenda. I doubt that Mr. Brenner would contest our decisions."

Everyone consented, deciding that Ceil should serve as chairman. As each child was discussed, she reviewed the original evaluation and family history and summarized the developments in treatment or therapy.

I talked about classroom behavior from September to May and described progress in learning both on a daily basis and by test results.

I felt confident about recommending Julie for transition. "We could try her first in a regular math class. That's a strong area for her. And she tested third grade, sixth month in reading on the Metropolitan Achievement Test. That's a big jump from first grade level, which she scored in October."

Ceil discussed her contacts with the parents and how much more accepting and better able they were to handle Julie. "At first they didn't see the relationship between her difficult behavior and the early separations from her mother and foster mothers. As they began to understand the origins of her anxieties and fears, they felt less threatened by the symptoms, which in turn are greatly decreased. There's been a good chain reaction in the whole family."

By unanimous vote, Julie was to be tried in regular class until the last day of school. If this transition went smoothly she would return to her local school in September.

Kevin, on the other hand, was seen as more disturbed than we'd originally thought. "The child has been atypical since he was an infant," Ceil said. "Although the neurologist found no signs of organic defect, psychological tests still suggest this may be a factor. Doctor Bialek's diagnosis is ego disturbance. There's also something vague about these parents," she added. "I've been seeing the mother all year, but I'm no closer to understanding the dynamics of the situation."

Ceil and I both requested that Kevin be returned to Transitional Class in September.

One of the administrators disagreed. "I understand, as Mrs. Craig has said, that this boy now expresses himself more freely, but both academic and emotional growth seem limited. I think we should offer his place to a child who's capable of making more progress."

"But we can't put a ceiling on Kevin's potential," I argued. "It's hard to present evidence of his improvement; we've just laid the groundwork this year. I feel we have a responsibility to continue."

The vote was seven to two that Kevin should return.

Jonathan's case was less controversial. It was a pleasure to report his accelerated progress in both reading and arithmetic. Although he'd entered the class as a nonreader, eight months later he tested on fourth-grade level.

"Marvelous," Miss Silverstein shook her head appreciatively.

"He's not ready to work in a group," I added, "but that's coming, too."

"His problems, as we have said, are still serious," Ceil summarized, "but he's come a long way for a child who couldn't be contained in a classroom last year. And the parents have benefited from marital counseling, so the family situation is more stable. I think Jonathan's a good candidate for a second year in our program."

Everyone agreed.

The discussion about Eddie was sad and brief. Ceil had just talked to the social worker at Green Valley. "They'll definitely admit him in June. We'll have a letter of confirmation soon. Mrs. Craig and I will start preparing Eddie, and I'll continue to work with the mother."

The planning for Douglas took longest. There was chuckling around the table as I described his behavior over the year. Their reaction encouraged me to continue, perhaps longer than necessary. But I was serious about the recommendation. "Douglas needs more time to consolidate the gains he's made. He isn't ready to move out."

To my surprise, it was Ceil who took issue. She reviewed the reasons for accepting this child without being able to work with his parents.

"We were interested because of his superior ability. Obviously his anger and insecurity interfered with his learning, and his school behavior was so aggressive and disruptive that we wanted to know more about the depth of his disturbance. I've been seeing Douglas for a year. The remarkable gains he's made in impulse control indicate that his earlier behavior was in response to his life experiences and not triggered by any emerging psychoses. I think he's benefited as much as possible from Transitional Class and should be tried in a regular group."

"He'd require a hand-picked teacher, both for now and for next year, when he returns to his neighborhood school," said Mr. Curnane, the junior high principal. "And we'd want to be sure he's not in a team-teaching situation in the fall. This youngster needs to relate to one adult."

"That's true for Julie, too," Miss Silverstein said. "Changing teachers is fine for children who are ready, but lots of kids get lost in the shuffle."

A young social worker, Doug Watson, leaned forward, pointing with his index finger. "Let's be realistic. There are limitations on how carefully picked the teacher can be. At Central School I assume there are three teachers at his grade level. Is any one of them ideal?"

"As a matter of fact, yes." Miss Silverstein said. "The oldest of the three, Muriel Flynn, offers the structure and support Douglas will need. He'll know his limits. At the same time, she's flexible and understanding."

Ceil, who had been taking notes, rested her pen on the lined yellow pad. "As for next year, assuming Douglas and Julie return to their neighborhood schools, Mrs. Craig and I will meet on a regular basis with their teachers. Before school begins, we'll make specific suggestions to the teachers and caseworkers involved."

"Well, I'm in favor of his moving ahead," Mr. Bentley said. "Could we put it to a vote?"

The others nodded. I felt nervous. My hands were cold. I rubbed them under the table.

"I don't know what a vote has to do with the way I see him." I tried to sound objective. "It's a question of whether he's ready, and failure now would be a terrible setback. I want to keep him until I'm confident he can succeed."

"There's such a thing as holding on too long," someone said softly.

The decision was eight to one. Douglas would go.

Supper that night was of necessity a quick affair, just tuna sandwiches and "Auntie Claire soup"—named for my sister who had first served the children noodles in tomato bisque. When the dishes were done, Ann and Richie returned to the dining room table to work.

Some of the salesmen from Bill's old company were treating him to dinner to celebrate the completion of his book. He had mailed in final corrections that morning. Bill invariably protested my going to evening meetings, and I was relieved that he wasn't home to see me rushing out, particularly since my attendance tonight wasn't compulsory.

I chastised myself for reneging on a personal pledge not to let the job interfere with family hours. But tonight no promise took precedence over the agitation I felt about Douglas' leaving my class. I needed to get out.

Dr. Bialek was addressing the Association for Children with Learning Disabilities. By eight-fifteen I was sitting next to Ceil in the rear of the crowded high school auditorium. He gave an interesting talk on dyslexia, a frequent cause of reading failure. I was glad I'd come.

The meeting adjourned at ten. Ceil rummaged through her purse for car keys. "I'm taking you out for a treat. I have a feeling you'd like to talk about Douglas. Let's go to the Gallery."

It was nearby, but on a less traveled road, and neither of us realized the restaurant was under new management. The cozy pizza parlor was converted into a noisy roadhouse. We stood in the glow of the red neon sign, alternately flashing "Liquor" and "Dancing."

"It's too late to drive around," I said dubiously. "Let's go in." Ceil tugged at the heavy door, and we were suddenly blasted by amplified rock music.

In the dimness it was hard to see which tables were empty. "Try and find a corner," Ceil yelled, "where we can talk."

But we never did talk. Nor did we order. I think we spotted them at the same time. My hand on the door, I took a last glance back. The next number was slow, and Eddie's mother was wrapping her arms around Mr. Brenner's neck.

# CHAPTER 31

"Is that the boy who raised all the ruckus at the fire drill?" Miss Flynn asked Miss Silverstein and me indignantly. She went on to recall other events in which she had seen Douglas play a feature role. "I don't have enough problems in my own class? You're telling me I'm getting him?"

Miss Silverstein smiled. She spoke calmly. "Now, Muriel, it's just for these last few weeks. We need your experience to help us judge whether this boy's ready. Besides, I've seen what you've done for so many troubled youngsters."

"Huh!" Miss Flynn sat back. But she looked pleased.

Mrs. Tefft, young and pretty, was more enthusiastic about being chosen as Julie's new teacher. We worked out a schedule for the week.

On Tuesday, both she and Miss Flynn stopped in to meet the children. The rest of the week, each teacher sent one of her pupils to escort Douglas and Julie to their respective rooms for brief get-acquainted visits. Douglas and Julie were proud of the prestige and attention this plan afforded them. Eddie was angry. "How come those bastards get to go and I don't?"

On Friday morning at ten, Ceil took Eddie to her office to talk about a new kind of school. She kept him longer than usual, almost two hours, while I wondered anxiously how he was reacting. Only Jonathan and Kevin were with me when he returned.

Eddie smashed the door open with a kick. It banged against the wall, the glass pane rattling precariously. His arms were loaded with toys from Ceil's office—puppets, Play-Doh, a can of Lincoln Logs. He hurled them all across the room.

"You're all goddamn bastards!" he yelled from the doorway.

"If you and Mrs. Black think I'm goin' to a go-away school you've got your minds crossed up!"

Wild-eyed, he darted to the reading table, knocked it on its side, kicked all the chairs around, and tossed a pile of workbooks in the air.

"Eddie!" I called, hoping he'd listen. "Let me tell you about that school and why it might be good for you."

"Fuck you!" He was purple with rage. "I wish you'd die and burn in hell!

"You too, fart face." He yanked Jonathan's chair out from under, and the heavy boy crashed to the floor. Jonathan began to rock and moan, "Oooo-oooo."

"And I'm sick of you and your goddamn shoes!" He rattled the back of Kevin's chair, but Kevin, his cheeks drained of color, eyes bulging, clutched the seat and refused to fall.

Eddie completely lost control. He tore around the room screeching, his arms extended like wings. I couldn't chase him. He was too clever to be trapped and escaped my attempt to block him by crawling under my desk and out the front. Lying flat on the floor, arms in a sort of landlocked breast-stroke, he propelled himself to Kevin's desk and wrapped both hands around Kevin's left ankle. Then he pulled Kevin's shoe toward his mouth and began chomping on the toe, growling like a crazed dog. Kevin was trembling. I tugged Eddie by his pants from under the desk, but he kept his grip on Kevin's ankle, and Kevin was dragged to the floor. Stunned, he just sat there, blinking.

Eddie writhed and kicked, and I had to let him go. He was tearing around the room when Ceil appeared at the door. Her head bobbed as she followed his erratic course, then looked from Jonathan to Kevin, both still on the floor.

"I've come for Eddie," she said loudly. "We hadn't really finished when he left."

"Oh no ya don't!" He dashed under her arm and out the door. "I'm not takin' chances on any more schools. I'll run away if you put me in that fuckin' place." He ran down the hall, his voice fading. He must have gone straight to her office, because Ceil made an all's-well gesture, a circle with her thumb and index finger, then turned to follow him.

We were eating breakfast Sunday morning when the phone rang.

"That sounds fabulous," I heard Bill say, "but you've gotta be kidding. All right, we'll do it. Meet you there by two."

I wondered who we were meeting and where. Bill, still in his blue terry cloth bathrobe, was grinning when he returned to the table.

"Everybody up! Those who'll be ready in one hour are flying to Chicago with me for the day."

"Daddy, stop teasing," Ann squealed hopefully.

"That was my publisher. He wants us all at the Booksellers' Convention for the afternoon."

Screaming with delight, the children scattered to get ready. "I've never been in a plane before!" Ellen cried.

Thrilled, though barely believing it was happening, we left the airport at noon and not too much later were circling O'Hare Airport in Chicago. The publisher greeted us in the lobby of the Blackstone Hotel, then led the way through the crowded convention hall. He stopped before a giant display featuring Bill's book.

"I wanted your family to see the booth," the publisher said. "We expect Bill's book to be a big success. Congratulations!"

Eddie wasn't on the bus Monday, and Ceil called the office later to say he and his mother were at Green Valley being interviewed.

Exhausted from our fast-paced trip, I was grateful for the easier day.

Douglas and Julie seemed to be progressing well in their new classes, and although Kevin was moody in their absence, Jonathan was blossoming. He began talking about astronauts, moon shots, and space ships, and together we read on the subject.

On Tuesday, Eddie was better than I'd expected. "I saw that damn school and I'm not goin'." But he spoke without conviction and paused as if anticipating rebuttal.

"I was real scared," he said later. "All the kids looked at me. I got to see where they sleep and where they eat. Those lucky bums get hot lunch, and even Jell-O too."

"It sounds like the boys get very good care, Eddie."

Dear Mrs. Craig,
I want to thank you but I don't know what to say except thank you for everything.

Love, Julie XOXO XOXO XO XO XOXO

"Yeah, well I'm not goin', so cross that idea off your brain." When he'd finished reading he lingered by the table. "Did ya know they're gonna build a swimming pool up there?"

Douglas' grace period, in which a child is uncertain of, if not intimidated by, a new situation, lasted till midweek. When more was expected in Miss Flynn's class, he began to falter.

"I'm getting concerned about him," she said in the teachers' room at lunchtime. "He wouldn't work at all today. Owes five problems for tomorrow."

I sat beside him that afternoon. "Let's look at the work for your other class. I'd like to help you."

"That's my business." He folded his arms obstinately. "And I'm not doin' it now."

"It's my business too, Doug. I want you to do well in Miss Flynn's room."

"Will you get off my back!" he snapped. Then after a long perusal of the ceiling, and each of his fingernails, he added; "Look, I didn't mean ta hurt your feelings, but can't ya have some faith? I'll do it myself. Me and Kevin are gonna play checkers now."

Julie was still in Mrs. Tefft's class. She'd been invited to stay for art and music, and had come hand in hand with her new friend Patty, to ask my permission. "I'll be back by two." She hugged me. "I wrote ya a letter."

Kevin never looked up from the checkerboard, but watched from the corner of his eye as Julie and Patty skipped out the door.

Jonathan and Eddie were constructing a helicopter with the erector set. I stood near them and read Julie's note.

The next morning, Thursday, Julie arrived first and reported that Douglas ate all his lunch on the bus, something he had done before on particularly anxious days. Hoping to prevent a major disruption, I waited for him in the hall. Seeing me, he pulled his yellow turtleneck collar even higher. The others filed between us as Douglas confronted me.

"Listen," he rasped, pointing to his swaddled throat. "I have this bad cold, see. I'm gonna stay in our room all day. These kids are used ta my germs."

"Miss Flynn won't mind your cold." I put my hand on his shoulder. "It certainly came on suddenly. Were you able to do those examples?"

"I did my homework," he looked me in the eye. "But I left it home."

"Doug, did you really do it or not? Is that why you're upset today?"

"The reason I didn't do it was I have this cold!" He shrugged my hand away. "I don't give a damn what you say."

For the first time in months, he and Kevin moved their desks to the corner.

"I'm gonna get in trouble," he murmured later to Kevin, "so I won't have ta go. Watch this."

"Help!" Douglas stretched the collar of his turtleneck up over his face. "Who turned off the lights?"

By chance, Miss Silverstein stopped in at eleven, when Douglas was due to leave. I scribbled a hasty note. "D's reluctant to go."

She nodded and approached him slowly. "I thought we could walk to Miss Flynn's together, Douglas. I'm heading upstairs too."

"No, thanks," he said quietly, not budging.

She picked up his hand. "I was so sure you'd keep me company."

He rose reluctantly, shuffling his feet. "Okay, I'll go. Who'd wanna stay in here? Douglas glared at me. "Who'd wanna stay with the nut teacher?"

Douglas' name-calling had only begun. But as he rejected me, his relationship with Miss Flynn improved. He began leaving notes on my blotter: "teachers are the dummest things" and "ole teachers our beddar."

Miss Flynn would chuckle over his comments and soon extended his time to two hours. Best of all, he kept up with the work.

While he and Julie were gone, a new relationship developed

between Eddie and Jonathan. It started over a mutual interest in space flight. Together they made a cardboard rocket. Eddie was still volatile and quick to turn on Jonathan. "Not like that, dummy! Why don't ya sit down and burp like ya used ta?" But he wanted Jonathan's friendship and most often was kinder.

Kevin now worried me most. He had begun to fall apart. At first I attributed it to Douglas' absence, but soon I realized it was more serious. He even looked disorganized, scuffing on the counters of his shoes, leaving pants unzipped, shirttails out.

He often had a vague expression, and when I'd try to draw him out he'd stare right through me with no glimmer of recognition. His desk, once impeccably neat, was an unbelievable jumble of scrap papers, crayons, and books. Sometimes he'd pretend to hold a rifle, and I'd watch him snipe at me and each of his classmates. Going home one night, he'd dropped a paper in the hall. "Remember the gun," it read.

Ceil suggested a conference with Mrs. Hughes. "He may be responding to something in the home."

But the day before we expected his mother, I was startled to find Kevin's father watching me from the doorway. I'd no idea how long he'd been there. When I left the desk to greet him, his visual appraisal began at my feet and worked gradually up. He folded his arms and grinned boyishly.

"Heard there was some kinda problem, so I thought I'd save my wife the trip."

"Well the appointment's for tomorrow, and Mrs. Black wants to be here too, but we'd like very much to see you both then."

"Uh-uh." His smile faded. "She can't make it, and neither can I. Just wanna know what the kid's been up to."

I invited him in and we sat at the round table. He held my chair. I felt uncomfortable seeing him alone. He was trying hard to be ingratiating. But his lips drew tighter. "Look, I'll be honest with you. My wife's got enough on her mind without wonderin' what you and Mrs. Black are gonna say."

"We don't want to upset either of you, Mr. Hughes. We felt you should know that Kevin is having difficulties, and hoped you'd be able to help."

"He been telling some kind of weird story or something?"

"It's nothing he's said. In fact, I wish he could tell me what's bothering him."

Mr. Hughes closed his eyes for a second. He slumped back as if enormously relieved.

I talked about Kevin's behavior, showing his father the unkempt desk. "When a child changes so abruptly and will talk to no one, we are naturally concerned."

"Okay, doll." Suddenly Mr. Hughes was on his feet. "You've got my permission to hit him anytime. Thanks for everything." Whistling, his hands in his pockets, he strutted out the door.

I never saw Kevin again.

# CHAPTER 32

"This committee is meeting," Mr. Hanley said, "to screen candidates for September. You've met Mrs. Orgel, our new teacher, who'll have the nine- to eleven-year-olds. Since both teachers are getting aides, we're going to place eight youngsters in each class. Mrs. Craig has two returning, so we have fourteen spots to fill. I want to get started right away. The next room is loaded with teachers and caseworkers who have information on the children we'll be hearing about."

I looked around the table. Counting Mr. Hanley, Dr. Bialek, and the new teacher, we were twelve altogether, but still no Mr. Brenner.

As if he knew my thought, Jim Hanley continued, "By the way, Mr. Brenner won't be with us much longer. He was anxious to return to Maryland, so he's there now for job interviews."

Ceil caught my relieved look and smiled back.

For four hours we heard about bright children who couldn't learn, deprived and even battered children, and those who were too difficult or withdrawn for teachers to manage in a regular class. One girl's mother had been in and out of institutions since the child's birth. A seven-year-old boy insisted on wearing beads and his sister's underwear. His parents were frantic. Another boy, eleven, with an I.Q. of 135, hadn't learned to read.

Dr. Bialek made interesting comments on each case. "Obviously this boy's suffered some subtle damage. I don't like hearing about mothers who were on tranquilizers or any medication during pregnancy. An expectant woman should take nothing, not even aspirin."

By six it was obvious that we couldn't finish, much less select fourteen children.

"I'd like to suggest meeting at nine next Wednesday morning," Mr. Hanley said. "However it's the first official day of vacation, and you'd be here on your own time. I know some of you are starting jobs and going to summer school, but I think it's urgent that we let parents know as soon as possible what we have to offer each child. I'm sorry to ask for one of your few free days."

Without exception everyone agreed to the Wednesday meeting.

"I'm wrung out," Ceil said, walking with me down the long corridor in the old Administration Building. "I've never heard so many difficult cases, one after another."

"I feel the same way." We stood by the door to the parking lot. "But, Ceil, I'm concerned about something else. You know Kevin was absent Thursday and Friday. Well he hasn't been in this week either. I keep thinking of how strangely his father acted. I've been calling there at odd hours, but there's never any answer."

"Hey, don't sound so panicky! The parents could be away. Kevin might be with them or with a baby-sitter. There are lots of possibilities. She looked at me, then added reassuringly, "Call me if he's still out tomorrow. Then I'll drive over to the house and see what I can find out."

I buzzed the office as soon as the bus arrived and asked the secretary to let Ceil know that Kevin wasn't on it.

Ceil came right after school, looking harried and bewildered. "It was so strange," she said. "No answer there, and none of the neighbors seemed to have even missed them. 'They keep to themselves,' I heard over and over. Finally, someone told me Mrs. Hughes used to visit a woman down the street, but she was as puzzled as we are. I decided then to call the police."

"Oh, God, Ceil. Don't tell me something happened to Kevin."

"Well, the two officers got into the house. It looked as if they'd gone in a hurry—clothes dangling out of open drawers, a few things left in closets, even food in the refrigerator."

I felt frightened. "What do you think, Ceil?"

She frowned and shook her head. "The police don't know what to make of it either."

# CHAPTER 33

Tuesday, June eighteenth. The last day of school.

At first, Douglas and Julie had asked about Kevin often, but this past week they had been spending the entire day with their new classes. I was receiving glowing reports from Mrs. Tefft and Miss Flynn. Both children would return to their neighborhood schools in September.

All morning Eddie and Jonathan helped me carry books to the storeroom, collect paints and crayons, and take down papers and charts. Until today, Eddie had seemed almost relieved about going to Green Valley, but now, knowing that he'd soon be on his way, he was edgy and apprehensive.

"It's your fault, isn't it?" he asked, continuing to sweep the floor. "You're the one who kicked me out."

"You know that's not true, Eddie. You understand why that school's a better place for you."

"Sure!" He threw down the broom. "Because you're so selfish and critical. Admit it, goddamnit! You don't think I'm good enough, but you're keepin' that crazy fatso."

Jonathan had improved to the point of caring when he'd been insulted. He stopped polishing his desk and sat back pensively. "I never call you names."

"I'll call you anything I want. Freak. Bastard. Bum." Eddie began circling Jonathan's desk.

"Come on, Eddie," I shook my head. I wanted this one day to be pleasant for all. "Anyone can say those words, but what does it prove? Think about the things you've said you liked at Green Valley, and stop feeling angry at Jonathan and me."

"Don't worry!" he shrieked. "I'm glad—glad to get outta this stinkin' place."

School was closing early, and the bus was due at noon. At eleven, Douglas and Julie returned to clean out their desks. When they were done, I served cookies and punch at the reading table. We ate together for the last time, conscious that this whole year together would soon be a memory. I looked at each child.

Douglas gulped the drink and held his cup for more. "I miss my ole buddy Kevin today."

"I'm gonna miss everybody." Julie nibbled her cookie. She edged her chair until it was touching mine.

"I'll miss you all too. But I'll be seeing your new teachers next year, so I'll get to hear about you."

Eddie ate cookie after cookie but said nothing.

Douglas slammed his fist against the table. "Don't make bad predictions, Mrs. Craig. I'll always be loyal to Central. You sound like we'll never even visit here again."

"Visiting's not the same Douglas." Julie looked out the window. "We won't even know the kids."

Douglas stopped eating. "I guess I'll never get to play under the new lights in the gym." He sounded gloomy.

Jonathan smiled at me for the very first time. "I'm glad I don't have to worry about missing that."

Julie put both hands on her hips. "Just because you're getting retarded doesn't mean it's good to stay back."

"Now, Julie," I said, "You know that Jonathan is not really staying back. He's—"

"The bus is here! The bus is here!" Eddie leaped up, knocking over his cup of punch. "Quick! I gotta do something." He grabbed a paper, ran into the closet, and closed the door. He was out in a minute and dropped the paper in his desk. "There. I left ya a note."

Pleased, I went to speak to him, but he dashed by me and out of the room.

Julie threw away her cup and napkin, then flung herself at me, her arms clutching my waist.

"Happy vacation, Julie." I hugged her. She was quivering. "You go ahead to the bus. I'll be out to say good-bye."

That left Jonathan and Douglas, still at the table. "C'mon," Douglas was leaning toward Jonathan. "Make one last goofy sound, like you always used ta."

"Heck no!" Jonathan stood up and pushed in his chair. "Are you crazy? Do you think I wanna be in this class forever?"

While they were getting ready, I couldn't resist a peek at Eddie's message. Raising his desktop, I picked up the crumpled note and unfolded it slowly.

He had blown his nose all over the paper.

Sickened and discouraged, I walked to the door behind Jonathan and Douglas. Ceil must have driven over to say good-bye, I thought, seeing her standing beside Julie. Eddie was already in a rear seat by a raised window. Not wanting his upsetting note to be our last communication, I went to the bus and spoke through the opening.

"I got your note, Eddie. Someday you won't feel so angry. Come back and see me." I barely removed my hand before he slammed the window.

Julie kissed Ceil and me. Jonathan allowed us each a brief hug and hurried onto the bus.

Squinting in the sun's glare, Douglas extended his hand. "Well, it's been nice knowin' ya."

I clasped his hand in both of mine and looked into his expressionless face. It was hardest to say good-bye to Douglas, perhaps because he'd been the first and always so unpredictable. "Have a wonderful summer, Doug."

"Summa? Oh God! Oh God! Not summa! It's summeRRR. Can't ya hear the R?" He shook his head, hopped on the bus, and shouted out toward Ceil. "Help her, Mrs. Black. She still can't speak our language!"

The driver closed the door.

Ceil and I stood waving. I struggled to maintain a smile and call out a last good-bye, but my throat was hopelessly jammed.

Eddie was crouching. Only the tip of his head was visible. Julie blew an abundance of kisses. Douglas, leaning out perilously, waved both arms in a slow crisscross pattern. Jonathan didn't wave.

But through the window I could see him mouthing "good-bye, good-bye" until the bus turned the corner.

I was still waving when Ceil caught my wrist. "Hey, they can't see you. They're gone. El, I've got to get back to the office, but I want to tell you something. Let's go in."

I sat in my chair, wishing I'd had a few minutes to myself after the children left.

Ceil perched on Douglas' desk opposite me. "I had a call from the police station an hour ago." It was hard to focus on her words. I wondered why she had to tell me this now. "It was the same officer who'd been at Kevin's house with me last week. He thought we'd want to know. The mystery of their disappearance has been solved."

"Ceil, what happened to Kevin?" I shrilled, jumping up. "What are you trying to tell me?"

"He's all right. Take it easy. I didn't mean to frighten you. It's Kevin's father who's in trouble. Apparently he's the prime suspect in a series of robberies. He was extradicted last night. Being held at the county jail."

"What about Kevin?" I asked, slumping back to the chair.

"He and the mother are staying in California. That's all I know. Listen, I have to rush. Someone's waiting in my office. Sorry to have upset you, but I knew you'd want to hear. Will you be through by three? Meet you at Mario's for a last chance to talk."

Stunned, I watched her leave, then just sat, unable to complete the countless closing duties. I thought about Kevin's behavior just before he'd disappeared: the sudden disorganization, his disheveled appearance, his "remember the gun" note—all cries for help.

I began to work on the attendance records and supply sheets but couldn't stop thinking of Kevin and his troubled future. It was nearly time to meet Ceil when I finally finished, stacked the papers to bring to the office, and dropped the line leader's chart on top of the over-flowing wastebasket.

At the door I took a last look back at our room and wondered if anything of value had been accomplished there. Julie had left her aqua comb in her cubby. Eddie's desk was pressed against mine. Doug's was at a peculiar angle, and on a whim I went back to straighten it. The motion dislodged a scrap of yellow paper, which fluttered to the floor. Reaching down, I recognized Douglas' familiar scrawl and smiled, then laughed as I read and reread his final evaluation.

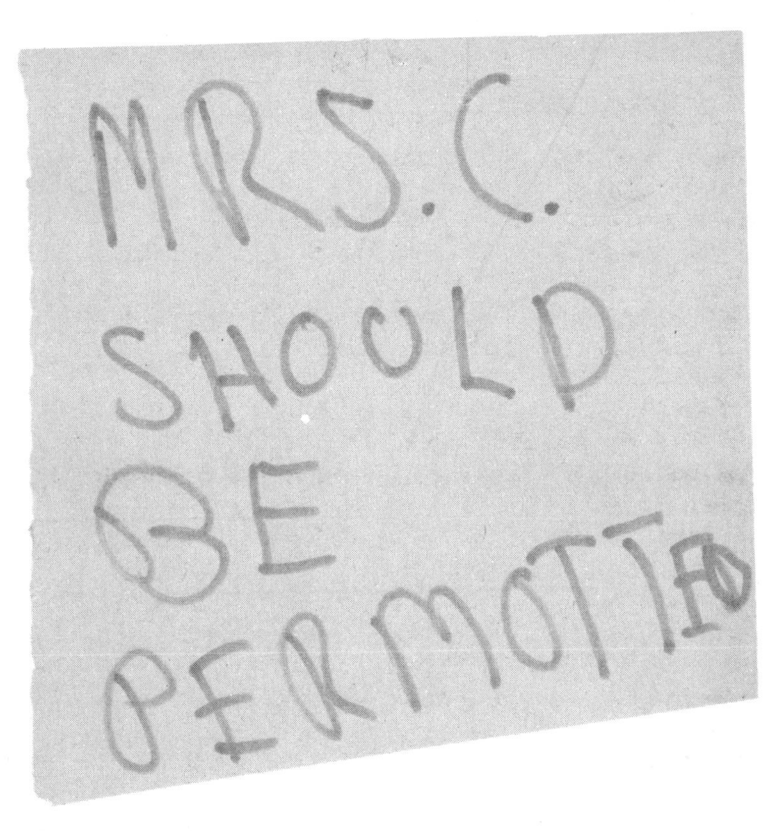